For every woman.

And to all the nice guys.

On a layover at Heathrow airport, my mother had written a stack of postcards to kill time. About to board the plane, she was still holding the postcards and realized that she had accidentally thrown our tickets into the mailbox instead.

The woman at the counter said she was very sorry, that there was nothing she could do. It was the weekend and the postmaster wouldn't be back until Monday. Not only would we be stranded for days, she would miss work and I would miss school.

I was six or seven at the time and I remember it as the only time I'd ever seen my mother cry. I always thought she'd felt defeated, but now I know, at the most, she felt a little foolish. It didn't last long. A minute later, she rolled up her sleeves, sniffled, looked at me and without missing a beat, said, "The worst they can say is no," and proceeded to teach everyone who was wearing a uniform what I already knew: you do not tell my mother no.

Within the hour, the postmaster came running, unlocked the box with jittery hands, handed her the tickets, and we were on the next flight home.

Every time I feel overwhelmed or that life is getting in the way of what I want, I am reminded of Heathrow airport, how my mother never settled, and that there is always, always, always another way.

Never give up.

Las Vegas, Nevada   July 25, 2015

Of all the places I had ever wanted to see, Seattle was it. Home of "Sleepless in Seattle," Starbucks, and Pike Place, and the notorious rain. Here I was, on the plane smiling from ear to ear. If I smiled any more, I could have cut glass, and we hadn't even pushed off the gate yet.

I admired the in-flight magazine cover, a picture of a bear catching a salmon from the stream with a single paw. Although I'd made a list of things I wanted to see, I was going to have to squeeze that in too. My arm could be twisted. I put the magazine back inside the seat pocket. All of a sudden, a screamfest erupted in the aisle aimed at the slumped-over kid in the middle seat next to me.

"How could you leave me? I was paging you and you were already on the plane?" the irate kid hissed from the aisle.

I use "kid" to describe both of them because neither looked a day over twenty-one and from what I could judge by the bloodshot eyes and alcohol wafting in my direction, I presumed they were just that; a day over twenty-one, dealing with the aftermath of partying days straight with nothing left to show for themselves except this sad attempt at getting on the plane.

Irate Kid shoved his bag into the seat and wrestled with the seatbelt.

"Sorry man," the slumped one shrugged helplessly. He didn't sound sorry at all, however, only like he wanted to sleep for a week. "You were taking too long. I didn't want to miss the flight, dude."

"Miss the flight?" Irate Kid huffed, exasperated. "You left my luggage in the bathroom, asshole! *I* was going to miss the flight! You were going to miss the flight?" he repeated, shocked. "Fuck you! You were going to leave me? Fffuck. I cleaned up after you all night!"

He stood up again as if he had somewhere to go and said, "We are not friends, Beau. Seriously, fuck you!"

Under any other circumstance, I would have let those two clowns duke it out. I did not talk to strangers on a plane. Most certainly not at six in the morning when all I wanted was peace and quiet to and think about all things Seattle. I had been dreaming of this for years and was a born tourist who had no shame in taking a million selfies in front of every flipping thing I'd retrieved from all the top ten websites, and couldn't afford to waste my time on distractions, precisely a moment as silly as this.

However.

I was on a book tour and for the book tour I had struck a deal with myself not to be boring-taking-care-of-business-and-putting-everyone-ahead-of-me-Jen. I was going to be outgoing and talk-to-everything-with-a-pulse Jen and seize-the-day-every-minute-of-it-period-no-matter-what Jen.

And with the mention of the name Beau, I suddenly recalled how funny that name was when it was paged over the speaker as I was running through the airport. I was running because I couldn't ever get anywhere on time and had paid attention to the name because I had only ever heard it before from one of the custodians at the airport where I worked as an air traffic controller. I had wondered why a specific custodian would be paged, when it turned out to be these two crazy kids who just now happened to have a meltdown beside me. As if this was the cue I'd been waiting for to add myself to the equation, I asked nonchalantly, "So, you're Beau? The one who was paged? I heard it."

"Yeah." He flipped his hands so carelessly in his lap that I knew without a doubt that if this plane were on fire he wasn't going anywhere. "I left because I didn't know what he was doing in there."

"Uh-huh," I agreed, because you couldn't argue with twenty-one-year-old hangover logic, and reached for the magazine again to gaze at a restaurant ad of a beautiful salmon filet on a plate calling my name.

"Ugh," Irate Kid plopped into his seat again.

"Sorry, dude," Beau said a tad more sincerely than before.

"It's good, man," he replied but locked his eyes on the seat in front of him.

I was definitely going to have a lot of salmon in Seattle, I smiled to myself. Breakfast, lunch, and dinner. Tourist style.

Seattle, Washington   July 25, 2015

Unable to fathom how it was so flipping cold in the middle of summer in Seattle when it was a hundred-whatever degrees in Las Vegas, I shivered and donned my hoodie I never flew without, and when that didn't help, found my phone and sent a text to my friend of twelve years who I worked with, and happened to grow up in Washington, *Sarah Louise! Why is it so cold in your home state? You did not warn me of this! And I see people in flip flops. FLIP FLOPS!*

I know LOL, she texted back seconds later. *I always travel with a fleece sweatshirt. You should be able to get one at the gift shop before you leave the airport. I've had to do that before. Did you pack a sweater?*

Yes. Three. And I have all of them on. I laughed, tried to recall a souvenir store in the terminal, and then talked myself out of going back in there because I was not buying a sweatshirt in July.

What are you going to do first? She asked.

Not sure yet. The line for the bus to get to the car rental is around the block and I didn't account for that. I'm getting hungry, and did I mention there are people in shorts and tank tops while I am shivering? I must have landed in the North Pole.

Can't wait to hear about your day!

I might freeze to death before I get to do anything.

LOL, she replied, and I crossed my arms for warmth and smiled at what a wuss I'd become after living in the desert so long that seventy something degrees was just too damned cold to sustain life.

It took over an hour to get to the car rental counter, but there was no line and I was waved over immediately by a man with a comb-over, friendly smile, and glasses.

"I know how to pick 'em," I said as I signed the two hundred fifty dollar lease agreement for "the cheapest car on the lot." "Why is it so expensive?"

"You picked the best time of year!"

"It's so cold though. You're kidding, right?"

"Believe it or not we're having a heatwave!"

"Well, I'm from Vegas," my giggle fell short. "Anything below seventy is too cold for me. What's going on here anyway?"

"Goodness, what isn't going on? Festivals, concerts, fairs, parades…isn't that why you're here?"

"Actually, I'm an author on book tour and I have a few signings at Barnes & Noble."

"What do you write?"

"So far, I have a memoir out. It's about my life in the military."

"Do you have a card? I'd love to read it."

"I don't." I sifted through my purse because, really, I loved it when people asked about my work but only wanted to be as accessible as Internet stalking allowed. I said, "What I do have is a few cards with the cover of the book on it. I was just trying it out. How's this?"

He studied the card, a grainy picture of me in my desert uniform, then slowly lowered it and dropped it on the counter in front of him like there was no way in hell he was ever going to read it.

"Good luck," he offered sweetly.

"Thank you," I said. Then pointed right and asked, "This way?" He nodded.

In the parking garage, I settled into the tiny white Chevy and typed Pike Place into my phone. I couldn't believe this was actually happening. Only twenty-two minutes away. So close I could taste it.

Once on the highway, I saw the city in the distance. The Land of Oz, my Emerald City, with its high-rises in the clouds, even more beautiful than I'd pictured. I hoped it would rain any second.

When I first moved to Vegas from New Hampshire sixteen years ago, rain was not a big deal. In fact, my first weekend there, I was at AutoZone, in line to pay for my hubcap dice (that I felt everyone in Vegas should have because it was so damned clever, when all of a sudden a clap of thunder and lightning took out the power.

But the unexpected storm wasn't to blame. The cashier had left his register and on his way out the door turned off the lights. More surprisingly, everyone followed him and I was left in the dark store by myself, staring at the people on the curb staring at the rain.

Seconds later it was over. Everyone trickled in and took their places in line or whatever they were doing before the rain had started and looked so solemn I thought they were nuts. That's what happens when you move to the desert; you miss the rain. Badly. And that's how much I missed it now.

Fearing I wouldn't be able to find parking close to Pike Place, I parked in the first lot I saw. Which was two miles away. It was so slanted that I couldn't resist taking a picture of my car. Across the street was a café called The Cherry Street Coffee House and it was as if all my tourist prayers had been answered. Nothing beats a local mom and pop shop. However, this mom and pop shop had a line out the door and no place to sit. I squeezed my way in.

Luckily, the line moved quickly and although my stomach felt like it was going to eat itself, everyone was in such a good mood that I wanted to be part of the vibe. I eavesdropped as the guy ahead of me joked about the three foot purple fairy pen he signed his credit card receipt with. Waving it around like a baton he said, "I bet no one tries to steal this thing."

"I would definitely try," I said. He and his girlfriend smiled at me.

"Quite a few people have tried, and failed because you can see it from space." The cashier laughed then took my order, a tuna sandwich and a coffee they were famous for, but with mocha.

In no time at all I had my food but no place to sit, unless I shared a table with a guy who looked like he didn't want to be bothered.

"Can I sit here?" I asked, twice, but with earbuds in his ears as he scrolled through his phone, he didn't look up until I slid my tray on the table.

"Do you come here often?" I tried again and he reluctantly removed his earbuds and said, "Huh?"

"Is this your usual hangout?"

"Nah, just when I get my haircut. It's right around the corner from here."

"That must be an expensive place if you get your haircut near Pike Place."

I was not about to admit that my "usual place" was Great Clips because my hair fell the same way whether I paid eight or eighty dollars, which Sarah Louise found both hilarious and ridiculous about me.

"It is now," he nodded. "I've been going to him for a long time and every time he switched locations, I followed him and now he's here. Now that I think about it, the price has definitely gone up."

"What do you do, if you don't mind me asking?"

"I work at Neiman Marcus. I'm the light and sound tech. Sometimes I have to hang new lights or set up different props, depending on what the store has going on."

"Sounds interesting." I visualized him swinging from the ceiling in a harness to adjust some lights. His messy hair indeed needed a trim.

"And you?"

"I'm an author on book tour. Actually, my first signing was cancelled today because of a computer glitch. My books were supposed to get in yesterday, but won't get here until Tuesday. They asked if I could stay longer, but I only have the weekend. So, all day today, I'm going to sightsee then go to Tacoma and Olympia tomorrow."

"My girlfriend wrote a book," he offered.

"Oh, wow," I said, but only because I hadn't pictured him with a girlfriend. "Did she publish it?"

"Nah. She works on it all the time then gets fed up and forgets about it for a while."

"I know the feeling."

"Who are you?"

"JG Debs."

"I've never heard of you." He typed something into his phone, scrolled through the internet hits, seemingly disappointed I wasn't more famous, and frowned.

"You have now," I smiled. Then my phone buzzed. He'd tagged me in a Tweet saying he'd met me and wished me the best in Seattle.

"Thank you, Eric Malor," I read his name from the screen.

"It was nice talking to you," he stood up. "I need to get going or I'm going to be late."

"Wait! What do I need to see while I'm here? Where's the best coffee and best place to eat? I mean this coffee is pretty good. I had to have a cup because the sticker on the door said *Barista Champion 2014*, but where do the locals go?"

"Hmmm. What do you like to eat?" He sat down again.

"I don't know. Everything."

"Pretty much everything that's good is around here, so you're in luck. Just up the block is a great Italian place. A Middle Eastern. Do you like Middle Eastern?"

I would have said yes except that my husband was of Middle Eastern descent and the thought of Middle Eastern food now turned my stomach. I'd eaten too much of it over the years from his family and didn't really want to think about him, or them now while I wanted to have the time of my life. I nodded politely.

"If you make a left out here and walk up the street a few blocks you can't miss it. And have you seen the Troll under the Bridge yet?"

"Never heard of it."

"Center of the Universe Sign?"

"No."

"You might as well see it since you're here. It's not far. It's definitely a local thing."

"What about the original Starbucks?"

"The original Starbucks is not the original Starbucks. The one on Pike Place is a tourist trap. You have to go past it and around the corner for the real one. But the best coffee place is there, I just can't remember what it's called and it's easy to miss. It's a walk-up window. Believe me, you have to have it."

"Italian place, Troll, Universe sign, Starbucks, walk-up window. Got it. Thank you."

"Have a good book tour."

"I will. And tell your girlfriend to keep writing."

Coffee in hand, Seattle was mine for the taking. I could have skipped to Pike Place, floated even, had I been able to shake the feeling that I should check out at least one of Eric's dinner choices. I couldn't stand the anticipation any longer.

And just like that, the magic however, unfolded. All around me people were holding bouquets, one more beautiful than the next, and although I didn't want to think about it, I was reminded of my wedding night and how amazing I'd felt when all the flowers from the reception had been lined up in the hotel room as if for a pop star after a concert.

Then the red Public Market Center sign came into view and someone hollered, "Step right up, you can catch it and have it sent wherever you live. We put it on ice, come on folks!"

It was just like how I'd seen in the training videos when I was a bank teller at Washington Mutual. The point of them was to show the "team concept" and that work could be fun. And as they shouted gleefully and indeed did play like a team, it looked like so much fun that I knew I had to see it live and in person one day.

Pushing my way through the crowd, I couldn't wait to catch a fish- that is right up until I saw the size of the thing. No wonder no one else had stepped up. No way in hell was I going to have a whale sent home to filet myself and eat for the next ten years. I backed up, delighted to take a picture of my feet with the golden hooves I noticed cemented into the ground, and then took a selfie with the glorious marketplace sign behind me. I could die happy.

Across the way was the Starbucks that wasn't really the first Starbucks. I would've tossed the coffee I was holding to get another because I didn't mind tourist traps, but the line snaked into the road and I couldn't waste an hour in line. Could I? No. No! I forced myself along, up the steep street where I found the Hard Rock Café, and took a selfie in front of the upside down guitar.

Growing up, I had at least twenty-something pins from around the world that I'd collected thanks to my mother's job at Lufthansa. I pinned them to the cloth roof in my car. While I was overseas in the military, however, I made the mistake of asking my brother to sell the car and he proceeded to a) forget to collect everything I owned from it and b) failed to collect any money in general which made me repo it back upon my return. I still missed those pins but didn't have the heart to start over.

Back at the market, I still couldn't find Eric's must-try walk-up window coffee place, so I hopped inside the marketplace where the only exciting thing to me was the Lamplight bookstore. Out the nearest exit, I ended up on a side road where I discovered a spray-painted astronaut statue that begged for a selfie, observed an outdoor cooking demonstration, and then became transfixed by a Ferris wheel in the distance overlooks Puget Sound. What a name, Puget Sound.

After a few more selfies with random statues, a whale's tail, and inverted umbrella, I made my way back to the car, typed 'Troll under the Bridge,' and was surprised it actually came up. It was only eleven minutes away.

In no time at all, I parked in what looked like a regular neighborhood with sidewalks, houses, and trees next to an overpass, and followed the few stragglers with cameras up the incline where I expected to see a garden gnome with a flaming red hat. Nothing, and I mean nothing, could have prepared me for the ugliness ahead.

I struggled to look at that thing through my camera phone without gagging at the one-eyed concrete blob crushing a VW bug. It was hard to believe the adjacent street was named after it, or even the apartment building off to the side. Who could live there? How did someone sleep at night knowing this monster was just feet away?

Getting out of there as fast as I could, I made it to the Center of the Universe sign-in less than five minutes. Now that thing was more up my alley; a pink pole with arrows pointing in every direction labeled with different places from all over the world. It was cool, as simple as that, and the first person who crossed the street didn't mind taking my picture, either.

The Space Needle was next, and as you can imagine, it was easy to find and easy to get to once I parked and fed the meter. The selfies of me pretending to eat it were priceless, and I couldn't hide my smile as I got in line to go to the top, until I found out it was a two-hour wait.

I was not waiting in that line and decided to walk around the base again, posed with Darth Vader and a Storm Trooper until the guilt ate me alive. How was I going to explain this to Sarah Louise? I'd come all this way without going to the top?

Back in line, I coughed up the extra twenty for VIP, which was absolutely worth it because I cut all the way to the front and right into the elevator. I'd been to the Eiffel Tower as a kid, which was awesome, but this, my dream actualized, was awesomer.

"Welcome to the Space Needle, I'm..." the tour guide said as we were shot into the sky at what *Spaceballs* accurately described as "Ludicrous Speed."

"Oh my, that's fast," an old lady held her chest.

"Yes, we just had renovations done." The tour guide smiled proudly, rambling off all the investments that I didn't hear but assumed only included the elevator cables and tried not to heave. The last time I felt this queasy was when I'd gone to the Grand Canyon and felt like I was going to fall in. "...And if you look over there, *Sleepless in Seattle* was filmed..."

But all I saw were clouds and I nearly cried thinking about how I wasn't going to see where Tom Hanks and his son had lived in that house boat or where they took the little boat to the beach and Meg Ryan watched them from the side of the road and knew he was the one.

Once at the top, I felt fine again, recognized some buildings from the top, and loved the one where an artist had painted an ant on the roof for my viewing pleasure. I wanted to ask someone about Sleepless in Seattle but felt silly. The tourist selfie camera, however, made up for it and I was able to send the picture of me with my hands outstretched, grinning from ear to ear, to friends via email.

Sarah Louise texted within seconds, *I haven't even been to the top of the Space Needle and I lived there most of my life!*

The line was so long I could have waited for you to get here! I said.

Lol, she replied and then *ten percent battery* flashed across my screen, my cue to get to the car, charge my phone, and get to my next destination, until I realized I hadn't packed my charger. It would have been a miracle had I not forgotten something.

About to curse up a storm because my trip was ruined, I GPS'd the nearest Apple Store, found one not too far away in University Village, and reasoned that I'd return the cable when I got back to Vegas.

University Village turned out to be an upscale outdoor mall so beautifully designed and perfectly landscaped you'd think you were walking in a catalog. As if they hadn't thought of everything already, each store had an umbrella bucket out front filled with beautiful bright blue umbrellas in case it rained. I had packed a tiny one, but I wanted to use a blue one and wanted to wait there until it rained in fact, had I not been so hungry.

I GPS'd my way back to the vicinity of Pike Place and soon felt like I was in an entirely different city when I saw that every sidewalk was now lined with couches, chairs, and caution tape.

"Excuse me! Hello?" I stopped the car in the middle of traffic. Cars drove around me without a single honk. Back home I would have been shot for inconveniencing traffic like this. "What is everyone doing with their couches on the street?"

"Where you from, hun?" she leaned slightly forward.

"Vegas!"

"See, I know you weren't from here, a-hm. Everyone from here knows when the Torchlight Parade is."

"The what?" I wished the light would turn red and stop traffic.

"Torchlight! We put chairs out the night before…"

"I mean there's actual living room furniture out here."

"Oh, yes, anything to keep your place, anything to get a good spot. We wait all year to see this parade and put chairs out the night before. You should definitely see it while you're here."

"I will," I waved. No way in hell was I waiting around for a parade when there was a city to explore and food to be had.

A few blocks later, I parked in the first open spot and fed the meter. I knew it was a bad idea to walk around in search of restaurants I didn't know the names of, especially when I was this hungry, but I considered it "being adventurous." Forty minutes into adventurous, I was ready to jump on someone's lap and eat the steak off their plate. I decided I'd walk into the very next restaurant and order everything off the menu.

A tiny Italian joint called Bella's was perfect, I thought. Heaven.

"Hello?" I called out after I sat down and waited and saw no one. I started hallucinating buckets of ice water, massive bowls of spaghettis, bread and butter and salads, and nearly cried at the thought of having to get up again.

Across the street was Local 360. I fell in love instantly. Magnificent distressed wood walls, oversized chalk menu by the door highlighting fresh salmon, and not one but two smiling hostesses who pointed me towards the bar because no other seats were available.

"Can I sit here?" I pointed at an empty stool next to a man in a suit.

"Go ahead," he said as he stuffed a receipt into his pocket and stood up. "There was someone there, but he left."

"Thanks." I sat down and moved the empty beer bottles to the side.

Behind the counter stood oversized wine bottles covered in globs of wax that I pictured fitting perfectly in my living room if I could have smuggled them out of there. I reached for a menu and heard, "Oh, I was sitting there."

"I'm sorry, that guy told me everyone left. I can move over." I glanced at the clean-shaven guy and noticed how built he was.

"Nah, I'll just take this one." He waved at the bartender for another beer. I said, "I'll take the salmon."

"What branch you in?" I noticed his camouflage hat on the counter.

"Air Force," he said, although I could recognize an Air Force uniform anywhere, even though it was the new camouflage color scheme.

"Me too. A long, long time ago." I paused. What were the odds of me, who'd written about my experiences in the Air Force, meeting a guy in the Air Force in a restaurant I wasn't even supposed to be in, in Seattle? "So, what are you doing here, of all places?"

"Flew in at five A.M. and my flight leaves at five A.M. tomorrow and I don't plan on being sober for any of it. You?"

"I wrote a book about the Air Force, actually. Well, it's more about my life, and it happens to be that I was in the Air Force, and I'm doing a few signings here."

"Cool."

"Thanks. So, what have you seen so far?"

"What haven't I seen? I took a shuttle bus from the airport and it dropped me off somewhere by the stadium. I wanted to watch a baseball game because I could hear the crowd but didn't want to sit by myself. Then I decided to have a beer in every bar along the way until I ended up here."

"I've been walking around this city too! And this restaurant right down the street, over there, no one would even look at me, so I came in here."

He took another swig and I wondered how plastered he was if it was now almost four P.M. and he'd been at it all morning.

"Where are you going tomorrow?"

"Korea."

"Ouch. Heard it's not the best place to be," I said, even though I knew nothing about it except that Sarah Louise had been there and she had loved every minute of it; when it came to tourist food stuff, she gave me a run for my money. Bugs on a stick? No problem. Live octopus? Pass her the Tabasco to splash on top. "It's for a year, right? And they fly you through Seattle to get there?"

"Yeah. I think it'll be fun and as long as I get back to Alaska, I don't care where they send me."

"I've always wanted to see Alaska. On a cruise or something, but now I've been in Vegas so long, I think I'd die of frostbite. I could barely stand it here today."

"You'll love it there. You have to visit me when you come."

"You have to try this salmon," I pushed the plate towards him.

"That's ok," he said. "I'll do dessert."

"Great! Order something."

"You order something."

"Chocolate cake?"

He wrinkled his nose and I flipped through the menu book again.

"Apple pie?"

"Apple pie works," he said, and told the bartender. "What kind of tourist stuff is there to see here besides the Ferris wheel? Did you see that thing?"

"Yes! I wanted to go, but I was kind of like you, why am I going to walk all the way out there just to sit there all by myself. Have you seen the Troll under The Bridge?"

"No," he replied. "Good choice on the apple pie," he said as he took a bite.

"I know, right?" I tried it too. "Ugliest thing ever this Troll. You have to see it. Actually, what are you doing after this? If you want, we can drive around for a bit. I have a rental car and I'll just drop you off at the airport after."

My words hung in the air as he said nothing.

"Or not. I don't even know what I was thinking. Sometimes, I just blurt things out and it's too late to take it back and I don't even know your name."

"Steve," he shook my hand.

"Jen. And I'm paying for your beer."

"Then I'll pay for the Ferris wheel. Now, let's go." He reached for his hat, committed. "Let me run to the bathroom since I'm feeling the beers. I'll be right back."

"I have to go too. See you up front."

But Steve wasn't up front when I left the bathroom. He was just a few feet away like a perfect gentleman and I nearly reached for his hand as if I'd known him for years.

"You're going to have to bear with me." I stopped cold as we left the restaurant. "Please don't think I'm an idiot, but I was so hungry when I parked that I have no idea where I left the car, except that it's this way. I think."

"I'm in no rush." He shrugged as if it wasn't a big deal, but something bothered him, like hanging out with a complete stranger was the worst idea ever.

"That's it. Wait. No, it is not." My cheeks flushed. I couldn't even look at him. "Oh, there. One more block. I see it. Here," I handed him my phone. "You navigate."

"A-ight," he agreed as we buckled up. "Straight then left."

"Wait 'til you see this thing," I said when I parked. "It's up there. I can't even look at it from this far away. I'm telling you, it's just hideous."

"Oh geez," Steve said once we were at the top.

"Want a picture?"

"No," he said as if I'd wasted his time. "We can go."

"Want to see the Center of the Universe Sign? It's right around, well, not too far from here."

Unimpressed, he replied, "Nah."

"Space Needle?"

"I saw it this morning."

"Good, because I didn't want to do this city twice," I laughed. "Ferris wheel?"

"Ferris wheel," he agreed and typed something into my phone and said, "Let's go."

A few minutes later, however, we were stopped.

"Oh shit, look at this traffic. I forgot about the parade going on today, and they're already closing down the streets, on top of all this construction. Find another way, maybe the highway or something," I said.

"I think it's closed. Look at all those cones," Steve pointed.

"Ask that cop."

"Keep moving," the cop said when Steve rolled down the window. "Parade."

"Is there no other way around this?" I shouted across the seat, but the cop only smirked as if to say Duh, *Torchlight Parade tonight*.

"This might be a bad time to tell you," Steve shifted uneasily. "I get really uncomfortable in traffic. I mean really bad, like we need to get out of this now, and I'm feeling those beers again."

"Okay." I panicked slightly since he was indeed a complete stranger and for all I knew he had PTSD or something, and what the hell was going to happen if I didn't get him out of this godforsaken traffic?

"Don't worry," I tried to calm him. "I have to go too. I'll park. I'll park at the first place we see, okay?"

"Okay." He slowly rubbed his palms on his thighs like he was doing a mental checklist and I thought *Just great, me and my great ideas, trying to live it up on book tour.*

"There," he pointed. "Just park over there. I think there's room?"

"Chinatown? Are we in Chinatown? Look at the dragons on those light poles."

"Yeah," he said, noticeably calmer because we were about to get out of the car. "We'll figure out where we are. I just really have to go."

"Me too." I paid the parking lot attendant and shoved the parking stub into my pocket, and we started jogging to the closest restaurant which was locked up, spray painted, and smelled of urine.

"Where to now?" I asked uncertain. "This probably isn't the best place for us to be."

"Down to the water," Steve replied. "We'll find something. First restaurant or whatever we see and we're going in."

"Deal. I'm about to pee my pants."

"There," he said a minute later. "Irish pub across the street."

This time, it seemed like he wanted to hold my hand as we stepped out onto the curb, but then both of us got distracted by the Ferris wheel in the distance.

"There it is," Steve said with awe.

"It's awesome," I agreed. As we got closer, I said, "There's an Ivar's here too. I promised my friend I would eat here if I saw one. Want to eat there after?"

"Fine by me," he smiled. As we balanced our way along the construction planks he said, "This whole city is under construction, huh?"

"Seems like it. At least the line is short for the Ferris wheel."

"My turn to buy." Steve bought the tickets and although I thought we were in line to get on the wheel once we entered a tent a photographer was waiting for us.

"Smile!" she waved. "Stand right there. Okay great, now do something crazy. You can kiss if you want."

"We just met," I pulled away. "I don't even know your last name."

Steve looked confused. The photographer said nothing as we walked out. I almost smacked my forehead. What was I thinking getting into a Ferris wheel, a very romantic ride, with a guy I didn't even know? Or was I supposed to kiss him because I wasn't going to see him again?

"I..." I started to apologize, but Steve shook his head like he knew what I was about to say, took out his cell phone, and said, "It's starting to rain. Let's take a picture."

"I can't get sick of this rain. It's beautiful to me."

Steve gazed out the Ferris wheel glass bubble we sat in, pensively.

"Do you have siblings?" I broke the silence.

"Sister."

"Brother for me. Are you two close?"

"I don't know," he shrugged. "I've kind of been doing my own thing. I love Alaska and being outdoors, and my family is in Iowa and I don't really go back much. Are you going to come visit me in Alaska?"

"I have no idea when I'll go to Alaska. My life is kind of a mess right now. My husband filed for divorce, said he doesn't love me anymore. Hasn't loved me in five years and yet we have two kids, four and one, and I'm probably giving you way too much information and should stop talking."

"But if you do come to Alaska, you have to look me up," he repeated as if he didn't give a rat's ass about my situation.

"Of course." I admired the raindrops on the glass. "This really is perfect. Want to take a selfie?"

He leaned in, smiled, saw the screen of my previous pictures, and asked, "Did you take a picture of yourself drinking coffee?"

"Yes. It's kind of my thing. I have a lot here, see? I get the same amount of complaints as I do likes on Facebook, and honestly, I think the pictures give enough information about me so that I don't have to get too personal or political. Know what I mean?"

"I think it's cool," he shrugged when the Ferris wheel stopped. "Ready to eat?"

"Inside or outside?" We stood for a minute. I wanted to get the hell out of there so I could fall into bed- my legs were killing me- but I didn't want to seem rude either. "I didn't know we'd have the option."

"Inside," he said steadfastly, as if the night wasn't over by a long shot.

"Happy birthday, man," the bartender said as he handed our ID's back.

"I didn't know it was your birthday! Why didn't you tell me?"

"It was yesterday," he shrugged.

"I was in the Air Force too," the bartender interrupted.

"Really?" I said dubiously. He was way too skinny and way too cool with that black slicked back hair to have been in the military.

"Combat controller," he nodded, but Steve and I looked at each other like *yeah right* and laughed.

"That little fucker was not a combat controller," Steve said when the bartender left to take another order.

"No shit," I sipped my water.

"You nervous about tomorrow?" he asked.

"No," I shook my head. "I never get nervous until I'm actually there. It takes me a few minutes to warm up of course, but that's what I love about this. It's different every time and I get to meet so many great people and they really like me, you know? Are you ready for Korea?"

"A year goes by fast." He paused. "Will you put me in your next book?"

"I haven't even thought about my next book." I sat back, thinking, why *hadn't* I thought about another book? "Yes. I will. *If* I write another, which I don't think I will, I will definitely put you in it."

"Good deal. And I'll see you in Alaska when you come to visit me."

Tacoma, Washington   July 26, 2015

My entire body ached when I awoke the next morning. I let the alarm blare for minutes before I forced myself out of bed and turned it off and reminded myself that this is what I had wanted, to be so tired that I didn't have to think about my real life. But how long could I keep this up?

I was grateful, at least, that I'd had the foresight to book the hotel in Tacoma and that I'd made the drive after I dropped Steve at the airport. By the time I'd gotten here, though, it was well after midnight and I became trapped by the chatty receptionist, who told me how she'd almost given away my room but knew I'd still show up, every busy night she could recount the last few months and weeks, especially when Justin Bieber was in town, and whatever else was at the tip of her tongue, until I finally cut her off and told her I had to get to bed for an early morning.

Once I arrived at Barnes & Noble I was ready for action. So was the barista as she poised her pen and asked, "Name?"

"Author," I replied jokingly. She hesitated, annoyed, and I almost told her that that was how I got in the zone because sometimes, just feeling good carried a bigger punch than caffeine.

Approaching the author table, my table which was by the front door, I beamed at the stack of my books and the poster of me behind them. I fished the Sharpies from my purse and then lowered myself into the wooden chair that fit me like a glove. I had accomplished all of this and just like Sarah Louise liked to remind me when I texted her that I was nervous, I had reinvented myself as an author. How many others could say they'd done that?

"You're the author?" A biker guy dressed in head to toe leather shoved his helmet under his arm and picked up a book. I nodded, about to speak, but he said, "That is so cool that you wrote a book. May I? I was in the Marines. Will you sign it for me?"

"I'd love to." I reached up to take it from him and wished they were all that easy. "Who do I make it out to? What did you do in the Marines?"

"I'm Dave. It was a long time ago. Now I'm here and taking it easy and enjoying life and that's all that matters."

"I'm happy to hear that. I hope you like it."

"I know I will. There's something about you." He paused. "I can't wait to read it. Take it easy."

"You too! Thank you, Dave!"

The next woman through the door either didn't hear me or didn't care as she walked past my table and I reminded myself to slow down on the caffeine and let them come to me.

"My daughter wrote a book," a man said as he passed by my table, picked up my book, and read the back cover.

"Oh, great." I waited for a comparison, for him to tell me her name to see if I'd heard of her or the book, but all he said was, "She didn't do anything with it though," then put my book down and walked away.

Next through the door was a two-chick SWAT team duo, dressed in black camo gear and so impressive that I stood up as they approached me.

"What's your book about?" The young woman with the cropped brown hair picked up my book.

"My life in the Air Force. How I joined, why I joined." I had it down to a one-sentence intro now, although I'd found out that it really didn't matter what I said. People either liked me or they didn't and decided to buy or not buy just for that reason. "Tell me about yourself, though. Are you SWAT or something?"

"No," the blonde with the ponytail said. "We're EMTs."

"And you're dressed like that? That's pretty exciting!"

"New uniforms," the blonde said.

"It's good," the one with cropped hair said, then I realized she was talking about my book and I smiled. Her name tag said Emily. Shyly she added, "I write too."

"Great!"

"Well, I used to write, I mean. I wrote a lot in school and I should pick it up again. I really want to but I haven't."

"Why not? What good is it sitting around doing nothing? It took me seven years to finish this book. Every time I had enough, I picked it back up again. Don't give up. You have something to say, say it. Ok?"

"Ok," Emily agreed. "Will you sign this for me?"

"I would love to." I signed it and handed it back to her. "Let's take a picture so that you remember this. I want you to keep writing and if you get stuck, please look me up. I'm everywhere on the Internet, okay?"

"I will." She shook my hand and said, "We have to get going."

I nearly fainted when I saw Sarah Louise's family walk through the door.

"You came for me!" I hugged them one by one.

"Of course we did!" Her mom handed me a box of candy from their hometown of Port Orchard. Every time she visited Vegas, or if Sarah Louise went home, she'd send one back for me. "We wouldn't miss this for the world."

"I love my fans," I joked, hid the candy box behind my purse, and said, "Let's take a picture for Sarah Louise."

"I love that you call her Sarah Louise," her Dad laughed.

"Can't stop now." I said. "And every time I call her that people are embarrassed they don't call her by her *real name* and then she has to explain that I'm the only one who calls her that, which cracks me up!"

"Sign one, please. For the family," her mother smiled. "We are so proud of you."

"Would love to." I drew hearts and smiley faces under my name and hoped to God they didn't read it with all my curse words in it.

"How is it being famous?" her brother joked.

"It's fantastic. Free coffee everywhere I go!"

"You should go to Port Orchard. A whole lot of nothing," he laughed.

"Actually, I can't wait to see it."

"I was kidding. Do not drive up there."

"I guess we'll let you get back," her mom interrupted when a man and his girlfriend approached the table.

"Thank you." I hugged them all. "I am so glad you came and saw me."

"Bye," I waved and said hi to the couple, a man in a baseball cap and his girlfriend, intently looking at my book cover.

"Tell me about the book," he said.

"It's about me in the Air Force. How I joined, why I joined, and everything in between. If you want to know what it was like for a punk kid who got kicked out of her house, had no idea what to do with her life, and joined to get out of her friend's basement, and how I became an Air Traffic controller, that's the whole journey right there."

"Will you sign it? To Mike?"

"Of course," I said as I opened the cover.

"Honey, take a picture with her." His girlfriend raised her phone.

"Get in here too," I said, and we took a selfie of all of us.

"I can't wait to read it," Mike smiled.

"I hope you love it," I replied, and that's when I saw him from the corner of my eye, roaming between tables with his girlfriend.

"Hi, excuse me. Weren't you at Pike Place yesterday? In the coffee shop? Cherry something? You were waving that fairy pen around, remember, and I was behind you and I made the joke about stealing it?"

Startled, he looked at his girlfriend and nodded, stared at my book cover and said, "Yeah that was me. What a small world. You're an author? Is that you on the cover? I was over there in 2004."

"Yes, I was there in 2003. What did you do there?"

"Medic. For the Army."

"So, you've seen some shit."

He nodded and I would have said more, told him that this wasn't that kind of story, that I didn't see what he saw but was still messed up for a long time afterwards, which was the whole point of the book. Everyone experienced the same thing differently while they were over there, and eventually he was going to feel better about it.

But sometimes it was just better to shut up.

"I wrote journals when I was there. It helped a lot."

"You still have nightmares?"

He nodded.

"So you stopped writing?"

He nodded.

"Write three pages a day, every time you wake up, about anything at all. That's what my first editor taught me. It will clear your head so that when you write, you can just write. Whatever you do, don't stop writing, ok?"

"Okay," he smiled, and seemingly relieved, picked up a book, looked at his girlfriend, and said, "She was at the coffee shop yesterday. Remember? I guess some things were meant to be."

Olympia, Washington   July 26, 2015

With two hours to kill before my next signing, I tried to GPS a brewery on my list that I'd promised another co-worker I'd visit. Although he couldn't remember the name of the brewery led me to Falls Terrace, which I passed twice before I realized that was it.

When I walked in, I saw the view to the backyard waterfall and boulders and fell in love instantly. I knew that was why he'd wanted me to see it.

It's still here, I texted, sending him a selfie of me with the waterfall behind me.

Hope I didn't give you a bad recommendation, he texted back. I sent him a picture of the cedar salmon I ordered, which arrived on a cedar plank on fire! And he replied, *I always loved it there. Kick ass on your tour.*

I'm on it!

Barnes & Noble was just a few miles away and I was ready to get the signing started. The sooner I got this ball rolling, the sooner I could get back home to my kids. Then I walked in and was crushed by the sight of two tables pushed together. It was going to be a long day after all as I studied the ridiculously tall man standing next to his table with his books piled on top. I was going to have to share the spotlight with that man and I never shared the spotlight.

It just didn't seem right to share a table. Who would want to talk to both of us at the same time? Why would I want someone to feel obligated to buy both or neither?

"Hi, I'm Jen, the author." I shook his hand and hoped he'd offer to move to the other side of the store. When I toured Reno there were at least two other authors, but we were spread out and we talked to each other cordially and compared notes when we got the chance. That was professional. This was a disaster.

"I guess I'm sharing a table with you." I prepped my Sharpies and failed miserably at sounding upbeat.

"Tom," he said, stone-faced, and we stared off into the distance. After a minute, he admitted, "This is my first signing."

"Don't worry." I glanced up at him, but was really looking for a manager who could explain this. But as he kept staring at nothing in front of him, like he was awaiting trial or something, I caved, remembering my first day in Portsmouth, New Hampshire, where the clerk behind the Nook counter walked me through what to do. I said, "I'll help you, nothing to it. By the way, how tall are you exactly?"

"Six seven," he said finally looking at me, which seemed awkward since I was poised perfectly at my table as he hovered above me.

"That's tall," I said stupidly, even though I was married to a guy six foot six and heard that question all the time.

"What's yours about?" he asked, looking at my book cover.

"Life in the Air Force. Yours?"

"I was a cop for thirty-three years. I was in the Air Force too." He cleared his throat as if that added more credibility.

"Hmmm," I replied, agitated because now it was even more ridiculous to have us next to each other and his book indeed looked interesting. I mean, who wouldn't want to read behind-the-scene, cop stories?

"What exactly do we do?" he asked.

"Well, you can sit down, for one."

"I'd rather stand." He turned around again.

"Okay, well, for one, I wished they had us closer to the front." I scratched my head. "This is too far back. We need to be able to greet people as they come in. We're buried behind calendars and coloring books here."

"Tell me about this one." A man with glasses suddenly approached us, picked up the cop book, and started asking Tom questions. Maybe I'd been wrong about all this. I tuned Tom and the man out and instead stared at the little girl who was wrapped around the man's leg. She reminded me of my little girl, who was waiting for me to come home.

"Oh, yeah? And how about yours?"

I came back to reality and smiled, "My life in the Air Force. How I joined, why I joined and everything in between."

"I'll take them both," the man said, and although I was grateful, I could tell he fell into the "obligated to buy both" category.

"See, Tom? You're a natural," I said.

"Hey!" Tom shouted, but not at me, at screaming, a two-year-old running down the aisle with his mother trying to catch him.

"Hey lady, I have a sticker for your kid!" Tom waved his arm and started after her.

"That's probably not a good idea," I stopped him.

"Back in the day, I slapped stickers on baby's diapers all the time. Moms love that."

"No they don't."

"Yes they do."

"I'm pretty sure they don't."

"I'm here to tell you they do."

I stared at him in disbelief. As a mother, I couldn't think of anything more annoying. As a human being, patron, and normal person just walking around, I couldn't think of anything more annoying.

"Okay, well, you're not going to do it here. Why don't you try sitting in the chair because it might be a little intimidating for people to approach us when you look like a wall or a tree."

"Do you think so? People tell me that all the time, but I'm used to standing."

"Now you're going to have to get used to sitting. You're not on patrol, you're an author. Let them come to you. Believe me, if they want to talk to you, they will. Some will buy just because you're here, or because you're an author or because after they talk to you, they like you. Every store is different. Every person is different. Enjoy it. Take it all in."

"You've done this before, I see."

"Yeah," I nodded, the last few months running together like water colors. And although I wasn't sure if I meant the book signings or life, I said, "It gets easier," and asked him, "Do you miss being a cop?"

"I haven't had time to. The writing and the grandkids keep me busy. Plus, my wife is happy I'm home."

"I bet you saw a lot of stuff." I smiled at the thought of a normal life, where I was a housewife and not the breadwinner, my husband coming home to me and kissing me on the cheek sweetly.

"I did."

"Tell me a story."

"There're so many." He half whistled and paused like he didn't want to say anything, but then it seemed to spill out of him. "Found some teens flipped over and dead after prom night. That was probably the worst. Having to tell their families. It's a small community where everyone knows everyone. Mrs. Harbinger, that was another bad one. Domestic disturbance call. I never liked those because you never knew what you were going to get. Usually, we could just talk John off the ledge, tell him to cool it, take him in for the night until he got sober. But one night was different. I just had a feeling I couldn't shake after she called the department and I promised her I'd handle it, thinking it was the same old song and dance until I got there. He was holding his rifle, crazy stare in his eye, the Mrs. shivering by the phone. He didn't like that I was there and I don't know what spooked him: me, my hand gently resting on my gun in the holster, or me telling him that it was all going to be alright if he came with me. He shot her right there. Damn shame."

"I can't imagine."

"You get used to seeing it. You just don't get used to all the bad news, all the time."

"How long have you been married?"

"Forty-six years." He was still in his daze. "You? Are you married?"

"Getting divorced," I said honestly.

Before I started the tour, I had made up my mind not to get too personal. Five minutes into it, I realized how absurd that was when I'd written a book about my life, and even more so when people started confiding in me. It became easy to open up, beautiful even, to be at the mercy of complete strangers.

"My husband left me after twelve years. I spent six months crying about it until I realized I had to get out of the house. So I called a few Barnes & Nobles to see if they'd let me do this and here I am."

"My daughter's husband just walked out on her," he said, and I bit my cheek not to cry. "What an asshole. And she just had a baby."

"I have two."

"He left her for someone else."

"Mine too," I said, remembering how I'd confronted him with the phone records on the computer and how he simply shook his head, casually deleted everything, and changed his passwords.

"Guys are so dumb these days. Never knowing what they have. He'll regret it, you'll see."

"Yeah," I muttered like I wanted to believe him, but what the hell was a little regret after you calculatingly destroyed an entire family?

"It's raining," I said noticing the drops on the window. "Was it supposed to rain today?"

"It's Washington. It's supposed to rain every day."

"I know," I said, although I didn't know at all. "I brought an umbrella and it hasn't rained since I got here, but I have a flight to catch." I glanced at my phone and my stomach turned as I calculated that we'd each only sold one book in the last hour and a half.

"You'll make it just fine." He waved as if it was nothing to drive in this rain but then suddenly looked at his watch and reconsidered. "It should only take you an hour, hour and fifteen, tops."

"My flight leaves at six." I had the sinking feeling I wasn't going to make it. "I don't see a manager, but tell her I'm sorry, I have to head out. Good luck, I hope you sell more."

"Here's my card," he said and I pocketed it, hoping to God he'd learned something from me and that all of this hadn't been a complete waste of time.

With all the confidence in the world I started the car. I was going to make it, just like Tom said, I just had to stay positive and ignore the crashing riptide on the windshield. I turned on the GPS and traced the entire red highlighted dead-stopped traffic route in search of a hole and then said fuck it. I pulled out of the lot and onto the flooded street. I had a flight to catch. I had to see my babies tonight.

Weaving through cars that refused to move through the downpour, I should have taken the obvious hint: if locals couldn't drive through this, neither could I. But I couldn't give up. It was unfathomable to me. Two days I had spent in Seattle. Two whole amazing days where I had all the time in the world to stroll through the rain, admire the rain, and not have an epic battle between life and death to get back to my kids because a year's worth of rain decided to dump on me now.

Slowly, I made headway, even though I was still projected to arrive ten minutes after my departure and I still had to return the rental. I prayed my flight was delayed, considered calling the airline, my tower, someone to relay the message that I was on my way and thought maybe, just maybe, the GPS was wrong, something was going to clear up.

It didn't.

At the valet, I stopped the car, wasn't even sure if I was in the right lane, grabbed my purse and carry-on, and shouted to a random kid in a uniform, "Keys are in there. How do I get out?"

"Elevator," he said, pointing in the direction I was already racing.

"Thank you," my voice echoed through the garage. I was going to make it! "You don't need anything right? I gotta go!"

He flashed a thumbs-up.

I flashed a thumbs-up back, already breathless and about to cry when I got out of the elevator and watched helplessly as the bus drove away. Motherfucker. I ran after it, but didn't last long and was forced to wait for the next one.

Too nervous to sit once I boarded the bus, as if that was going to make the bus go any faster, I thought my heart was going explode with anticipation. I pushed my way through the terminal after the bus stopped, cut to the front at TSA, made it through security, and nearly cried when I saw I was departing from the very last gate in the farthest terminal.

Sweat dripped from my forehead as I got on the tram, another time waster. Children stared at me in silent fascination. Why was I running through the terminal like that? I had to keep the hope alive. I was so close.

At the gate, passengers were in line about to board and I almost screamed with joy until I saw the flight was going to Chicago. Seriously. I checked the departure screen, I wasn't too far away, found the last burst of energy within, and darted.

"Oh my God, I made it!" I clung to the counter and tried to catch my breath.

"Actually, you didn't," the woman replied unapologetically.

"What do you mean, the plane is right there. You're kidding, right? Tell me you're kidding. Look at me, I'm drenched, I just ran through this entire airport and I don't even want to tell you what it took for me to get here."

"No," she smiled sadly. Surely, I was being punked. "The plane is here, but the door is closed. We paged you, but you weren't here."

"What did I miss it by? A minute?" I stared at the perfectly good airplane through the window, so close that if I waved, the pilot could wave back.

"Five minutes," she said as she typed something. "I rebooked you on the next flight, which leaves in two hours. Here's your new boarding pass. Have a nice day."

"Thanks." I shoved the boarding pass into my purse, found the nearest bathroom, changed my soaking wet clothes, and laughed because I truly did only go to the gym to run through airports.

How was your signing? Steve texted as if on cue.

Good, I replied, smiling. *But I missed my flight.*

Me too, he said. *I'm still in my hotel. Meet me. The shuttle bus drops you off right in front of the building.*

Flight leaves in two hours. I won't have time.

Two hours is plenty of time. Who said anything about serenading you all night?

Reno, Nevada   December 19, 2015

Before I could thank my friend Pat for picking me up from the airport, I slid into the front seat, held my phone up, and apologized, "I didn't mean to call you Sis, but I was texting Crystal and then I confused it with you."

"For the love of God, don't even think about calling me Mom," she snapped as she merged into the outgoing lane. "Call me Sis so I don't have to kill you. It sounds better."

"Okay, Sis it is," I agreed, took Chapstick from my purse, and hoped I'd be as spunky as her when I grew up. "Where are we going? Crystal had mentioned IHOP but I wanted to try a local place."

"Yeah. No way. Oh, Crystal. I told her that I'm not going there. There's a cute little place called The Stonehouse Café. I've always wanted to go and now we have an excuse to. She's going to meet us there. And remind me to give you the goodie bags for the kids. They're in the trunk."

"Aw, thank you, Pat. Have you seen Crystal at all since you've been back?"

"No. Shame on us. Well, me really." She paused. "I've been wanting to see her. It just didn't happen and there's no excuse since my schedule is more flexible and she lives right down the hill from me. I did try once before the surgery but it didn't happen."

"What surgery?" I was suddenly a little jealous that Crystal was in the loop and I wasn't, as if the three of us really were sisters and one preferred to tell something to one but not the other.

"I had this thing under my arm that I kept ignoring for years until a friend of mine told me to check it out because it got so big I couldn't fit into t-shirts anymore…"

"Like a golf ball?"

"More like an orange."

"Pat!"

"What? Who has time to go to doctors?"

"I don't know, but if I had a growth on me, I'm sure I would have it checked out."

"Yeah, well I had just recovered from knee surgery and wasn't in the mood," she said, not even kidding, which only made me like her even more. She was going to do was what she was going to do.

"This place looks great." I marveled at the small smooth stone house and wooden steps as Pat pulled into the Café parking lot.

"Let's head in, maybe she's already inside. I texted her before I picked you up and told her not to text me while she was driving."

Inside, the ambiance was everything I could want in a local place. A bar took up most of the front room. The other rooms had small tables and booths stuffed into them, giving the café that lived-in feeling, almost as if there were bedrooms in the back and whenever you felt like it, you just rolled out of one with pajamas on for mimosas and omelets.

"There she is," Pat said.

Crystal stood up from the table and waved. She really could pass as my sister, with her long blonde hair and sincere smile.

"What have you been up to?" I hugged her and scooted into the booth first, Pat and Crystal on either side of me.

"Same old," she said. "Although it's getting quite lonely in the office since they've let so many people go. It's just me and one other guy."

"One? My God, why?"

"There's not much left to research in the mines up here," she shrugged.

"Are you worried?" I asked, worried.

"Nah, not really," she said, upbeat. I swear, nothing could get this girl down. "It will just motivate me to start my own business."

"Also in the mining industry?"

"No way," she laughed. "Dogs. I'm really good with dogs. I used to train everyone's dogs in the office and did really well with it, until, you know, they let everyone go."

"Like the dog whisperer?" I joked.

"Better," she smiled. "I use psychology. The same you use with your kids. We take walks, like they do in packs, and I can teach them things like running on a treadmill."

"Really?"

"Really."

"I try everything on my kids and they don't listen to me. Actually, neither do pilots," I laughed.

"I understand them. It's easy."

"Good for you," Pat said. Our food arrived. "I absolutely love the idea. By the way, these are the best eggs I've ever had."

"Mine too," I said.

"I love this place," Crystal agreed.

"What's up with you, Pat? How are things at your job?" I asked.

"I make my own hours. It gets me out of the house and gives me something to do. My husband works long hours at the restaurant, you know?"

"Yeah." I nodded dreamily, because she had mentioned that when we first met months ago. I had pictured her in her little store, organizing the merchandise, and her husband always cooking. I admired them and wondered what it was like to be married to someone that long, to not have someone give up on you.

"How are you doing?" Crystal asked me, concerned. The look on my face must have given away something.

"You're going through this divorce gracefully," Pat squeezed my hand. Crystal smiled at me sympathetically. "You didn't feel sorry for yourself. You got back out there. Not many people can say they've done what you've done."

"Well," I laughed. "I don't know how graceful I was crying my eyes out everywhere, but I can't complain."

"How are the signings?" Crystal asked.

"I love it. I always say I'm a famous author who nobody knows and makes no money. It's good and I'm so busy, but it's kind of catching up to me now. Everything I had booked months ago seems to all be happening at once. I flew in from New Hampshire last night and I didn't even have time to do a signing. I was there to work with a charity group that I had met last time I was out there and they got me a TV interview, radio interviews, and I got to talk at schools. I mean, I'm still soaring from it now. It was really pretty incredible."

"It sounds incredible! I'm halfway through your book and I love it."

"Thank you, Pat!"

"Hmm, I bet it is beautiful in New Hampshire right now." Pat closed her eyes dreamily.

"I love that air," I agreed.

"The trees," Crystal added. "It's so green. Pat, I meant to tell you, I'm actually going back next month."

"Already? Feels like yesterday we were on the plane together," I said.

"This time I'm going for ten days. I felt so rushed last time, like I couldn't do everything I wanted to or see everyone I promised I would."

"I always feel like that too," Pat said, "no matter how often I go. I have to limit it to one or two friends, my mom. That's it. I don't feel badly about it anymore, either."

"Every time," I added my two cents. "It's like I have time to get Dunkins and then I'm literally running around all day saying hi to everyone."

Pat said, "It's true. And speaking of running around, I have to cut this short. Jen, I'm so sorry…"

"Please," I stood up with her and hugged her. Then Crystal did too. "No, really. I understand. If it hadn't been for you, I wouldn't have called Barnes & Noble and come up here.

We'll see each other soon. Next year? Same time, same place?"

"Or else," she hugged me.

"But we need a picture of us first."

"Definitely. Oh, no, girls, I'm getting the check."

"Pat!" I stammered.

"No way." Crystal agreed.

"It's not even up for discussion. I've got it."

After she signed the check, Pat said, "Now, let's get out of here."

"How about we take a picture out front?" Crystal suggested.

Outside, I hustled over to a woman who had just parked her car and asked her to take a picture of us.

"Until next year, girls. I love you," Pat hugged us. "Jen, the goodie bags."

"Okay," I followed her to her car, getting a little teary-eyed. The last six months had put me on a journey I never saw coming. Never had I felt so alive, so loved, so fearless and fearful at the same time. And Pat and Crystal were one of those reasons.

"See you next year," I said. I got in the car with Crystal, who was all smiles, as if nothing gave her greater pleasure than to drive me around when really, it was me who couldn't believe how lucky I was to have met her.

"Are you nervous?" She drove around the busy Barnes & Noble parking lot looking for a spot as I envied the shoppers.

I loved the holidays, the whole nostalgia of it all. Cooking all day and eating and eventually wrapping gifts. But I usually worked holidays and missed being at home, and now with the divorce none of it was going to be the same, not even daydreaming about it, and it made me sad.

"I can't believe all these holiday shoppers. I always need a few minutes to warm up. Wow, it does seem like a lot of people. I think there's an extra week to shop before Christmas this year. Last year there was one week less and everyone seems to be making up for it."

"I can't wait to see you in action." Crystal said.

"Ha, I don't know how much action there is. It just kind of happens from one moment to the next."

"This is your table?" Crystal marveled at the sight of my table once we entered Barnes & Noble.

"It's awesome, isn't it?"

"Before you get started, will you sign one for me?"

"Oh, Crystal. You don't have to."

"Of course I do. I was waiting for you to get here before I bought it. I can't wait to read it. I'll just hang out over there, okay?"

"Okay, Sis," I said, and as soon as my butt hit the seat, a shy teenage girl with short messy hair approached me.

"You. Wrote. This?" the girl stuttered.

"Yes." I smiled encouragingly.

"I have. Tourette's." she chirped suddenly.

"It's okay, take your time."

"This. Is so. Cool. How. Much. Is. It?"

"I think twenty-two."

"I. Don't. Have. Enough. I'm. In. College."

If it had been one of my local author signings, I would have been able to give her the book, but giving her a book now would be stealing from Barnes & Noble. I wanted to hug her. I remembered my college days well, when I had zero dollars to my name, and the fact that she was willing to spend her money on me made my day.

"What are you studying?"

"English," she frowned. "It. Looks. So. Interesting. I'm. Sorry. I. Can't. Buy. It. Today."

"If you have Kindle," I whispered, since Kindle was Barnes & Noble's competition and considered taboo to say aloud, "you can find my book there. It's a little cheaper, okay?"

"Okay." She nodded as if she wanted to cry then said, "I'm Sorry." Then I left. For a few minutes, I watched people coming in and out of the doors, walking around and people, reading from lists. I even spied on other authors in the store that I hadn't expected to be there. I made a mental note to talk to them later.

"Excuse me, where's the bathroom?"

"Back corner," I pointed.

"And do you know where the maps are?"

"Umm, they are usually right around that area," I pointed the other way. "And if you're looking for something different to read, here's my book."

"Oh," the woman studied the cover. "It looks sad, is it sad?"

"Yes," I nodded. "But it ends well." I put my hands in the air like ta-da.

"I'll take it," she smiled. "Will you sign it for me?"

"Of course."

"Katherine."

"Enjoy it."

"I will."

"You wrote this?" An elderly man with a comb-over, little pot belly, and thick Russian approached me.

"Yes. It's about my life in the Air Force, how I joined, why I joined."

"I no want to buy your book. You should hear my story." He picked up my book then dropped it back on the stack, disinterested. "I'm not going to buy this, but my family, let me tell you about them. They survived Russia and fled and I wouldn't be alive today if they hadn't made it. You should write my story. What do you think about that?"

"You mean to ghostwrite your story?"

"Yah, ghost write."

I knew the term because I'd looked into ghostwriting after years of struggling with my own manuscript and having it not come out as I'd envisioned. Then I discovered the cost and decided it was me who was going to have to fix it, no matter how long it took.

"Usually, you want to know the style of the author first."

I said that only because I'd read the book *Open* by J.R. Moehringer and became fascinated with the idea that Andre was such a good writer. Doing a little more research, I found out that Andre Agassi had loved Moehringer's writing style after he'd read "The Tender Bar" and had sought Moehringer out to write his book. It made perfect sense.

"If you like my writing style, then of course I'd write it for you…"

"It was 1929," he talked over me. "And it was cold and snowing and they left their town because they no longer believed in the politics and decided to flee to America. Isn't that something?"

"It is…Come on over," I waved at a woman who looked like she didn't want to interrupt and wished I could tell her to please, please, interrupt all you want.

"Yah, yah, I know you busy, but my story," the man said. "And they crossed mountains and towns and people helped them out…oh, maybe I should come back later. I see I'm in the way. Can I email you maybe? You should really hear my story. Would you write my story? Do you have a card?"

"I don't. I'm sorry." I glanced at my book. "But I'll write my email address on the inside cover, how does that sound?"

"I didn't want to buy anything today."

"That's fine." I shrugged and he stared at the cover, opened it and pushed it towards me, and smirked, "Okay, okay, I'll buy it. You got me. Make it out to Nikolai."

"I hope you love it."

"Yah. You'll hear from me."

"Jen, this is my husband," Crystal said coming up to me. I hadn't realized two hours had already gone by already. "Honey, this is Jen, who I've been telling you about."

"Hello, husband." I shook his hand, suddenly I missed having my own husband. It was always nice to be introduced as his wife or he as my husband. "It's so great to meet you."

"You too," he said quietly. Then, as if he didn't know what else to say, he kissed Crystal on the cheek and said, "I'll see you at home, okay?"

"Okay," she waved. To me she said, "I already read the first chapter. I love it."

"Thank you," I said, shoving the Sharpies into my bag. "We can actually head out if you want. My time is up and I did pretty well." I indicated Crystal's husband, who was heading out of the store. "You two are cute together. I miss having one of those."

"We have our ups and downs."

"Who doesn't? At least he's sticking around. That says a lot." I stared absentmindedly at the dark sky.

"I wish you didn't have to leave so soon."

"If I lived here, we'd hang out every day."

"I love you," she hugged me after she dropped me off at the Departures curb.

"I love you, too. Thank you for everything. Thank you for driving me around today. I'll call you soon."

"I can't wait."

I waved one last time, went into the terminal, and only had several people ahead of me at TSA. At the gate I found out there was only one other flight scheduled at this time and mine was delayed an hour, which wouldn't put me in Vegas until way after midnight.

"Could this week get any worse?" A woman in a black suit was talking to a man whose black pant leg was covered in mud.

Scanning the boarding area, everyone seemed to know each other, like I was interrupting an office Christmas party.

"It figures," the man answered her. Next to him stood a guy with coffee stains down the entire length of his shirt. Maybe it was a zombie party.

By some coincidence, the woman in the suit sat next to me on the flight. She was at the window seat and I was in the middle. Unable to contain my curiosity, I asked her, "Excuse me? Is this some kind of office party?"

"You could say so, right Ted?" she spoke over me, to the man in the aisle seat.

"What business are you in?" I wasn't going to let up now, even though I could tell she didn't want to answer.

She studied me for a moment and then she said, "We are part of the Nevada State Legislature. And what was supposed to take two days to decide on took over five because we got snowed in and we didn't have a change of clothes, which is why we all look like this. Some of us tried washing our clothes in the sink and it's been a disaster. I'm so grateful to be going home. It's just been the week from hell."

"Nevada State Legislature?" I almost choked at my luck. "Who do I talk to about Veteran Affairs? I've been trying to get into the VA to teach writing classes for PTSD vets and I just keep getting the runaround."

"Right over there." She pointed out a man whose shirt was untucked and hanging out of his suit coat. "He can help you with anything you need and if he can't then you get back to me and we will figure it out, sound good?"

"It sounds exactly like what I need. I can't thank you enough."

Wilmington, Massachusetts   December 16, 2015

All I had to go off of was a note that read *Paul Panera Bread, outside Boston* that I had written months ago. At one of my earlier signings, a guy representing the charity *Ipods for Wounded Veterans* had asked me if I was interested in radio and TV time and after I'd nodded, he dialed someone (Paul) on his phone and handed it to me when it was still ringing and I agreed to represent his charity and he agreed to help me promote my book in return.

I stood outside Panera Bread, trying to figure out if it was Paul every time a car drove up. He texted he was going to be late, but I wasn't sure how late.

"Paul?" I approached the Ford Explorer after I watched it idle for a full minute after it pulled into the parking lot.

He rolled down the window and said, "Jennifah, good to meet ya," with an accent as thick as my Dad's. His hair was completely white, making him appear older than I initially thought. "Sorry ta keep ya waitin'. I forgot somethin' and had to run back. Get in, get in. I'll drive ya around so it's quicka. No sense in ya gettin' lost. Busy day today. I hope ya ready."

"Do you mind if I run to the car and get my bag? I wasn't sure if we were going to eat here or if you were giving me an itinerary of where we were going. I just need to do my make-up. I don't like flying with make-up on."

"Su'a," he nodded. "But hurry."

Pam! I texted. *I'm sorry I can't see you right now. I didn't know what to expect, but I guess he has the whole day planned out for me. I'll see you tonight?*

Inside the bathroom, I leaned the phone on the sink, applied mascara and eyeliner, and then texted Sarah Louise, *I'm here!*

How's Boston? She replied.

I wanted to say my usual "fabulous," but this wasn't going to be my usual visit of Dunkins, hanging with friends and family, and doing a signing here and there. This was more like a hostage situation. *Met Paul, said we were going to be busy. Trying not to get too excited and trying to just go with it. You know how hard that is for me.*

You'll be great. Can't wait to hear all about it!

I replied with a smiley face then fake smiled at my reflection. This was what it was all about, right? Not having a plan. Not being in control. Letting go and going with it. Being nervous, feeling out of place, adapting. And so, I had no choice but to let go and exhale.

"That was fast. Good," Paul said when I climbed into the SUV. "What a day I have planned for you!"

"Bring it," I said, putting my hands together excitedly.

"Ya gonna eat those words," he laughed. "Ya head's gonna spin. You have a cah? You can leave it here. Ya not gonna know where ya drivin', believe me this is easier. Let's see, what's first?" he tapped the steering wheel. "We need to get more fliers and I want you to meet everyone the charity works with...Statehouse for lunch...and of course you'll meet all the board members tonight at dinner."

"Okay," I said nervously. He had told me about the Statehouse, but I hadn't taken it seriously. Was I really that important to have lunch at the Statehouse?

"He'a, talk to him," he said, handing me his phone.

"Hi?" I asked, startled, flattered, and aghast that he'd let me talk to whoever was on the other end. "Yes, I'm the author. Thank you. I appreciate that. I can't wait to meet you too. Ha, I will. Bye."

Slowly, I handed Paul his phone back. "He said to tell you you're a real pain in the ass and to make sure to tell you that."

"Oh, I'm a pain in the ass? I'm a pain in the ass? He's a pain in the ass. Don't worry, we'll get him back later. You'll meet him tonight with all the other board members and you can tell him yaself."

"I don't know if I want to do that."

"The hell you don't," he shook his head. "Don't worry, I'll tell him first and you'll see what a pain in the ass he is. We'll get him."

"Oh, there's a Dunkin Donuts. Nothing makes me feel more at home than Dunkin Donuts. Can we get coffee? I'm starving and I just love their coffee. They just don't make it the same in Vegas."

"Of coss." He parked the Explorer and said, "This is my usual place anyway. The office is right down the street." He told Doris behind the counter *and* the two patrons inside who he actually knew how busy we'd be, making me wonder what exactly I had volunteered for.

Where the hell are you? Pam texted me. *I took the day off and I'm at the house waiting to see you!*

I am so sorry, I gritted my teeth at my lame response. Wannabe author on book tour who couldn't make time for her best friend who graciously let her stay with her every time she was in town? There really was no apology for that. *I thought I was going to see you first and meet this guy somewhere else, but I'm tied to a schedule now. I don't know when I'll be back tonight. Believe me, I am very sorry!*

OK, she replied. I felt like an asshole.

"Go ahead and go inside," Paul said when he parked in front of his office fifteen minutes later. It was some kind of veteran service office that looked more like a wood cabin. "I walk a little slower."

The log cabin theme continued on the inside. Wood panels covered in military paraphernalia like TGIF restaurants, large windows with a view of the street on one side and trees in the back, and a large oval table cluttered with boxes of pamphlets.

I waited for Paul to introduce me to the five or six people in the room, but all he said was, "This is the author," and I went around and shook everyone's hand as he looked for something on his desk.

"You can sit here," a woman my age with long dark hair said as she waved at me.

"I'm Stacy," she shook my hand vigorously. I found that most people didn't have a good handshake so I always loved finding people who had one.

"What do you do here?" I was a little mystified since no one looked younger than ninety-five.

"Right now? I just have some down time. I'm about to head out. But usually I take care of the veteran homeless population in the area. Make sure they have a place to live, help them find a job, or sometimes, well, I have this one guy Jim, he says he likes it better sleeping in the woods and so I check on him to make sure he doesn't need anything."

"That's pretty fantastic. I don't think we have anything like that in Vegas."

"You don't?"

"I don't think so." I thought back to when I got out of the military and had no idea who to turn to except a recruiter who'd given me his office number if I'd wanted to join the Reserves.

"Tell me about your book," she said excitedly. "I can't wait to read it."

"Oh." I struggled to follow up her heroic tale with the one about me struggling with what I wanted to do with my life. "It's about my time in the Air Force, from basic to Air Traffic School, and getting deployed and coming back."

"I did Air Traffic too," she smiled, and I almost told her that I knew there was something I liked about her. "But I didn't make it. I always regretted it."

"Don't say that." I bit the inside of my cheek, wishing I could tell her I hated my job and that the sacrifice hadn't been worth it, but it had been. Trying to sound upbeat, I added, "You're doing something amazing. I can't imagine anything more rewarding."

"I know," she shrugged. "I love what I do. It's just sometimes I wonder, you know? My sister is still in, she's an officer. She loves it."

"My brother was in too. But we only did four years and we're both in Vegas now. Do you have kids?" I noticed an engagement ring and felt a twinge of jealousy.

"Two. One from a previous marriage and then my boyfriend has a daughter. I love her so much. It was like it was meant to be."

"I have two, as well, and an ex, and I don't know what the future holds but when I hear stories like yours it makes me think that there really is someone out there for me." I wanted to hug her. Fuck ex-husbands.

"There is." She smiled, stood up, and said, "It was so great to meet you. I have to run, but I can't wait to read your book."

"I'm glad I met you too," I said, and Paul shouted from across the office, "Jennifah. I got what we came fah. Let's go."

"Want me to help you carry that? I work out." I reached over to grab the heavy box from him, but he wasn't having it.

"Get in, get in," he tsked. "Next stop is the Senior Home. I want ya to meet a few of the board members. Ya'll see them at dinnah, but I want to show ya what we do there."

"Okay." I sipped my coffee and stared at all the trees as he drove. There was nothing more beautiful than New England. I was about to relax into a daydream about moving up here, or at least having a house I could get away to and write, when he suddenly handed me his phone again.

"Yes? Hi, I'm the author. I can't wait to meet you either. I'm very excited…Paul? Oh, no, he's fine. Very nice. Yes. Ok, bye."

I hung up and wondered why everyone kept calling him a pain in the ass.

"You know who that was?"

I shook my head.

"Great guy. Fellow teamstah."

I made a note to look up "teamster" since all this affiliation stuff sounded a little mafia-esque and I thought maybe I shouldn't get so comfortable.

"He's in Flaw-rida. He runs the oar-ganization from there. So, if ya ever in Flaw-rida, ya call him. I'll give you his numba and ya can tour there. Sound good?"

I nodded, knowing I'd have to make the call. At the beginning of this, I had told myself I wouldn't stop until I heard "no," but the "nos" just weren't coming. I was going to be on tour forever.

"Why does everyone think you're a pain in the ass?"

"Aw, shit? Did he tell you that? He's gonna get it lata'. He's lucky we don't have time right now. Come on, we're he'a."

Up the stairs, I opened the door for Paul and was introduced to Darla, a woman with a kind smile, glasses, and short wavy hair.

"It's great to finally meet you," she said as if she'd been expecting me. She shook my hand and asked, "Is he giving you a hard time? You just tell me if he does."

"No, no, he's great."

"He paid you to say that, didn't he? Paul!"

"What? Naw," Paul said. He didn't come with us as I followed Darla down the hall.

"This is where we make the bracelets. We sell them for five dollars. That helps us fund a lot of the things we do here. I'd give you one but we're all out. Hang on, I'll be right back. I've gotta see what Paul is asking about…"

Sitting there, I wondered when all the action was going to start. Without me realizing it, several people had trickled in and sat down close to me, and before I knew it we were exchanging names and stories, and I told them how I came to sit before them, how I'd written my book, and the journey I'd been on the last few months.

I was captivated by them. And they were captivated by me, just for being myself.

"We gotta go." Paul's face poked through the door.

"Sorry," I excused myself.

"Don't be sorry. It's Paul," Darla joked. "But you are not leaving before we take a picture of all of us." She handed Paul her phone and he almost dropped it.

"I don't know how to use this blasted thing."

"Aw, for goodness sakes, Paul." Darla looked at me. "You don't even know what's in store for you, do you?"

Smiling, I got back in the car.

"Aw'right, State House," Paul said. "Ya going to meet the Secretary of State of Veteran Affairs and then we'll do lunch there."

"And what do I tell the Secretary of State of Veteran Affairs? I mean, I looked him up, he's from my Dad's home town and he was in the Marines, but otherwise I don't know what to say to him."

"Tell him about ya book. He knows a little bit about ya. And then he'll tell ya about the policies in Massachusetts, what they're doing for veterans all around the State. He won't have a lot of time. He's very busy. It took months to coordinate this."

Now I was convinced I wasn't that important.

"You know Tom Shae? He did a book signing right ova there and they fawgot to orda his books." Paul pointed at a building in downtown Boston but I missed it.

"They did? What did they tell him? What did he do? I had the same thing happen to me, but he's a big time published author!"

"He demanded he get paid anyway. So they had to cut him a check. Ya shoulda seen the line for people wanting to see him. All they could do was back orda the book, so he hung out and signed whatever people wanted him to sign and he took pictures with whoever wanted pictures."

"I want to be just like Tom Shae," I said, wishing the publisher had to cut me a check for what happened in Seattle and in Phoenix.

"That is magnificent," I said, stunned, as we drove up to the Boston State House. I took a picture of the gold dome with my phone as he parked. "I can't tell you how many times I've driven by it and never, ever did I think I'd go inside."

Paul smiled as if he knew something I didn't. "Wait 'til we get inside. I have a special parking space, they'll actually pahk this faw us."

"Welcome, Mr. Paul. Jennifer." The car doors flung open and we were greeted by two young, energetic guys in suits.

"We need an itinerary, Adam, do you mind writing one up?" Paul said as we made it through security.

"No problem, Mr. Paul," Adam said.

"Right away," Jeremy added.

"Make yourself comfortable, Jennifer," Adam pointed at the leather sofa in the office.

"Is there anything I can get for you? Water? Coffee?" Jeremy asked.

"Water. But I can get it, it's no problem."

"Right away," Jeremy said, disappearing.

"How are things, Mr. Paul? Are you giving Jennifer a hard time?" Jeremy asked once we were all seated.

"I wahrned her," Paul joked.

"Mr. Secretary might not be able to make it," Adam shook his head.

"It's no problem, really." I stared at all the diplomas and VIP handshake pictures on the wall, feeling as if I'd met the President. "I am so honored to be here."

"I called the office and he's in a meeting, so we shall see," Jeremy called over from the other office before appearing seconds later with a copy of my itinerary. "This is for you, and Mr. Paul, here is your copy."

It was official, I was now more important and busier than I'd ever imagined. If Paul was running things for me in Vegas I'd have been famous already.

"When Tom Shae was here, the Secretary couldn't make it," Jeremy shook his head.

"Oh, yah," Paul chided in.

"I'm reading his book now." I pulled out *Unbreakable* from my purse and watched as all of them lit up. "So far, it's fantastic. I wish he was here so I could ask him questions."

"I've been meaning to read it," Adam said.

"Me too," Jeremy agreed.

"Great book. Great book!" Paul was ecstatic.

"Let me check on him again," Jeremy said, excusing himself.

As the chatter erupted in the hallway minutes later, I knew someone very important was approaching. I stood up nervously. How could I have only worn a turtleneck? I rolled off the flight and came here looking like this?

"Jennifer, good to meet you," Mr. Secretary shook my hand, unbuttoned his suit coat, sat down across from me, and joked with Paul, "Are you working this poor girl to death?"

"She said she could handle it," Paul shrugged.

"Jennifer. Tell me a little bit about yourself," Mr. Secretary started, and although I'd had months of practice, it was tough to spit it out.

"I was in the Air Force where I learned Air Traffic, which is what I currently do in Las Vegas.

I actually looked you up before I flew in and I saw that you were a Marine, which is impressive. And how's this for a small world? My Dad is from your hometown."

"Really," he nodded. "So, do I know him?"

"I don't think so," I laughed.

"Okay, so you work, have kids and have time to write a book, that's impressive." He paused. "Let me tell you what Massachusetts does for our Veterans…"

I was fascinated by the entire operation and couldn't avert my eyes from the secretary. He had taken time out of his day to explain policies that were downright impressive, press conference worthy, and I sat there like a deer in headlights not even taking notes.

Before I knew it, Mr. Secretary stood up again, posed for a picture with Paul and me, wished me luck with my book, and disappeared. Paul looked like he was about to fall asleep now that all the excitement was over and I wished I could have traded places with him, but Adam whisked me from the room and said, "Time for our tour! We're already late!"

I didn't see Paul again for another two hours, after it was getting dark and we were escorted back to his car.

"The tour was amazing. It was really the chance of a lifetime and I can't thank you enough."

"Sorry. I couldn't hang. Just too much walkin' already today."

"I can't believe it's almost time for dinner. It's already dark out," I said, knowing I wasn't even close to being done with Paul for the day and worried what Pam was thinking about me right now.

"Tomorra's even busier," he said, dialing someone on his phone. "Not all the board members are going to make it tonight, but maybe you can come back in May and we'll get some more events together."

"Sure. Okay, we'll plan it when it gets closer so I can see if I can get the days off for work," I said, pushing away all thoughts of falling into bed and sleeping for a week.

"Here we are." Paul parked in front of what looked like a gigantic castle. It was called "The Lodge."

"It's beautiful," I said.

Although it was loud inside, Paul introduced me to everyone at the table, including his wife, and I felt honored to be a part of their usual get-togethers. I pulled out the only empty seat and Paul said, "This is Michael. He's also an author," then joined his wife at the head of the table.

"Jennifer! So good to meet you! Tell me, who is your publisher?" Michael asked.

"I am." I tried not to sound pretentious, but it was the number one question people asked me on tour. That and how I actually did it. "It took me seven years to finish my draft, but the whole time leading up to it I was contacting publishers and agents and no one seemed to bite, so I went with Amazon. Their customer service is fantastic. They helped me with everything."

"And the tour, how did you manage that?"

"I petitioned to get into Barnes & Noble and had to republish with their accepted publisher. I'm considered an "Indie" author.

"Remarkable."

"Thank you, but I think it sounds more remarkable than it is. All I did was research a little bit after I heard a local author on NPR one day. Then I emailed NPR and got on a local morning radio show a few months later. Then I asked myself well, how do I get into the library? And then I petitioned to get into the library and made a speech there and then wondered well, how could I get into Barnes & Noble? I then applied there and petitioned magazines and newspapers to review me. Some worked out, most didn't, and then the more people I met, the more connections I made, and here I am."

"I just love your story," one of the wives next to me, said as she leaned over and touched my arm.

"Thank you." I smiled because nothing made me feel more special than the women supporting me through all of this. Not to say that the men didn't surprise me with all of their support, but I'd always heard that stupid saying that women don't support women and I had found that that was absolute bullshit. All the women I'd met on tour embraced me. If I told them I did it myself or that I was divorced or that I had two kids or was in the military, it didn't matter. They approached me and were in awe of me, which made me in awe of them and made me feel so absolutely, ridiculously empowered, special, and invincible.

I glanced over at Paul, who winked at me. How could I ever repay this man for taking me under his wing and making me feel like I belonged here amongst a group of strangers?

Townsend, Massachusetts   December 17, 2015

All I could think about was sleep when I rolled up next to Paul's car in the parking lot.

"Ya late," he said. "Those kids are counting on us."

"I'm sorry," I offered weakly. It was four A.M. my time and he hadn't given me a second to breathe the day before. Thank God the line at Dunkins was long or I would have gotten coffee and been even later.

I flipped down the passenger side visor and applied make-up. I'd skipped it at Pam's, thinking I could make up some time, but obviously it hadn't helped. My eyes looked tired, but I was grateful to be here. Full steam ahead. No looking back.

"What do I say to a middle school, by the way? I think I told you I haven't given any school speeches yet…and you know my book has foul language."

"Ya know Thom Shea's book? It's filled with foul language he was a Navy Seal for crying out loud. Ya fine."

"I wish I could have met him. I would love to ask him about some of the stories in his book. Do you remember the first story? Oh my God, I wished he'd elaborated more. That bike race was the best thing ever, the one with the friend who gets a blister on his butt? I mean, can you imagine that?"

"Great story," Paul nodded. "As for his speeches, though, he does more motivational speeches. And you, you should talk about your experiences as a woman in the Air Force. They wanna know what it's like. I'll staht first, talk about the charity and what we do, hand out brochures and keychains so they can take that home and show their parents, and then we collect their 'Dear Soldier' letters. We'll take them to Walta' Reed Hospital when we go in a few months. Don't worry, if you run over I'll cut you off."

"Don't worry about me running over. I can give a thirty minute speech in three minutes. I talk very fast. Especially when I'm nervous. But okay, good, you're like my manager and I'll look for your cues. I can do that." I pictured myself on an auditorium stage looking for him in the crowd as he tapped his wrist "Time!"

"Aw, for Gawd's sake!" He slammed on the brakes. "Look at this traffic. We're gonna be late!"

"We still have an hour." I tried to calm him because it was obviously my fault, but he stayed tense for at least another twenty minutes until we saw Boston police standing around a barrier in front of a street they'd blocked off.

"All that hoopla faw nothin'."

"We'll make it, right?"

"Ya," he said. And we did, with ten minutes to spare.

Unloading the trunk in a parking lot no larger than a courtyard, Paul replied to my shock with, "That's Boston for ya," and handed me a rolled-up banner as tall as myself. I then followed him and his collapsible dolly inside.

"So glad you're here," the receptionist greeted him. She told him which classroom to go to and he said, "Have a nice day," so casually, as if he was here every day, making me wish I could be as calm as him.

But I was nervous as hell. More and more kids appeared out of nowhere, from every hallway, nook and cranny. I needed a good opening line, but was drawing a blank. What could I possibly say to these kids about being in the military and war?

"He'a." Paul handed me flyers to pass out which was good, very good, because the kids thanked me like I was handing them Jell-o, making me believe that they were going to love me no matter what.

"Aw'right kids," Paul started when he was at the front of the class. "In the essence of time, we need to staht. You rememba me, I'm Paul, Chairman of *Ipods for Wounded Veterans*, an aw'ganization dedicated to bringing all the latest gadgets to the most severely wounded soldiers at Walta' Reed Hospital in Maryland. Along with your "Dear Soldier" letters, thank you for writing those..." The kids and teachers gave themselves thunderous applause. "...Yes, those letters brighten those soldiers' days, ya have no idea, so keep writing them!"

"We have more for you to take with you, Paul," one of the teachers interjected cheerily.

"Great! So, now without further delay, is author Jennifah, who served in Iraq and will tell you all about her experiences."

"Thank you," I waved. This was my largest crowd, and although they were only eight or nine, I didn't want to disappoint. "Hi, I'm Jen and I am so happy to be here in front of you today. Who knows what an Air Traffic Controller is?"

I should have let at least one of them answer when at least ten hands shot up, but I was still nervous and immediately rattled on, "Okay. Wow. When I was your age I had no idea what a Controller was. I had flown my entire life because my mom worked for an airline and I never knew that people talked to airplanes to keep them safe. When I joined the Air Force I still didn't have an idea. Does anyone know what the Air Force is?"

"Like the Army!" a little boy shouted after I pointed at him.

"Yes! Except that in the Air Force, we deal with a lot of planes and I got to talk to them, bring them in and out of airports. I did that when I was in Iraq, too. Except that when I was there, there weren't any houses for us to stay in. Picture a huge sandbox. That's where I was, nothing but sand, and we had to build tents and bring planes and people in for our mission. After six months I got to go home, but because I was overseas for so long, I had forgotten what it was like to be me and I had a hard time getting used to doing normal things like shopping, driving, and hanging out with friends. Eventually, I ended up getting a dog and he helped me get out of bed every day, and after a while I felt better and wrote a book about my experiences."

Looking at Paul, he nodded his approval, glanced at his watch, and asked, "Isn't that something kids? Do ya have questions?

"Did you kill anyone?" one boy shouted out before his teacher reminded him to raise his hand.

"No," I smiled. What the hell were kids watching these days? "Yes, you," I picked one from a sea of hands.

"What kind of planes, uhm, did you see?"

"The most common ones I worked with were F-16's and F-15's. Those are fighter jets. Then A-10's, they are really, really loud, like brrrrrrrrrrrt- you can hear them from miles away. Their nickname is "warthog" and that's exactly what they sound like. Also, large cargo aircraft, which is what I flew in to get to Iraq and back, and also helicopters."

"Do you know karate?"

"No. I didn't learn any combat. I did learn how to shoot a rifle, though."

"Great questions!" Paul said, which got me even more amped up. "Just a few mo'a. We need to get goin'."

"How many pushups can you do?"

"Not many. I do not like pushups. At all. I struggled in basic training, especially with pushups. I never did any exercise before I joined and so I had a hard time with that. I cried every day. But I got better every day too and I knew that if I didn't give up, I would be okay."

"How did you learn the job?"

"After basic training, I went to Mississippi to Air Traffic School for a few months. After I passed that, which was very hard, I went to Las Vegas, which was even harder. But just like in basic training, I learned something new every day and eventually, everything started to make sense."

And just like that, it was over. Paul said, "That's all the time we have faw now, kids. Thank you!" and I was almost disappointed. I felt like I could have gone on for hours.

Thunderous applause followed and although I wanted to take it in for a little while longer, the kids picked up their chairs to leave and Paul needed help packing up his stuff.

"Excuse me, can I ask you something?" one of the teachers tapped my shoulder. "First of all thank you for your service and that was really great…" Suddenly all the teachers were around me. "…And I know you didn't know this, but I have a little girl in my class who cries every day no matter what, and when you said that, she looked at me and lit up, so thank you for that. You made her day."

"I'm glad," I said, getting a little teary-eyed. "I'm glad I made a difference at all. And otherwise, everything was appropriate?"

"Oh yes, you were great!"

"I, uh, have a friend who was overseas," the next teacher said. "He was a firefighter and saw all his friends die, like had to collect their body parts, and he's never been the same since. Do you have any books you can recommend on PTSD?"

"I don't have a book that I can think of." I suddenly felt like a truck had rolled over me. All that pressure to find the perfect answer because really, I should be an expert at this because now that I knew what PTSD was, thought that I had had it or at least shown very similar symptoms. "What I would say is, give him a journal and a pen and tell him to write three pages a day. That's how I started. Every morning, no matter what, first thing, three pages about anything: dreams, laundry, anything at all. And that will help clear his mind and maybe help him sort some things out."

"What a great idea," she smiled. The load from my shoulders lifted a little.

"We have to go," Paul said, handing me a poster. "Thank you, ladies."

"Thank you," they beamed.

"Thank you," was all I could muster from all the adrenaline finally coming down.

Loading everything back in the car, I said, "Paul, I did it. It was so much fun! I mean, did you see how excited they were and did you hear those questions? Weren't they the most random questions? And they loved me."

"Ya did good," he nodded. "Ya did good. Thawty-fo questions I counted and I had to cut you off."

"I can't wait for the next one, where is it again?"

"Townsend. A little ova an hou'a from he'a. Let's hope the weather doesn't get any worse. This one's a high school and ya'll have a little bit longa to talk, but I'll cut ya off for the radio interview. Ya'll need to find a quiet spot to do that. And tonight, don't forget, we have the TV interview at the station."

"Okay. I just need coffee at some point."

"You and ya coffee."

"Only if you can." I slumped into the seat, my eyelids heavy.

"He'a," Paul nudged me with the back of his hand and gave me his phone. "Say hello to…"

"Hi!" I said, starting to get used to Paul's surprise phone calls that seemed to occur as soon as my eyes seemed to close for a catnap.

"Tell him tomorra' we'll see him and he'd betta have his Santa Clause suit ready to go. We'll see who's a pain in the ass now, won't we?"

Boston, Massachusetts   December 18, 2015

It was just a few minutes after six A.M., and by some miracle I was actually going to make it on time today. I couldn't even think about how busy it was going to be, and how exciting really, or how good it was going to be to see my kids tonight. I stuffed my pajamas and toiletry kit into my carry-on, deflated the air mattress, and bunched up the sheets to take them to the laundry room.

Pam's bedroom door suddenly opened as if she'd been waiting for me.

"Oh, Pam, hey," I said. Her look told me I was dead meat.

"Where have you been, Jenny?"

"Pam, I'm so sorry, really. I know it sounds bad, but…"

"Seriously. All day you're gone and God knows when you come home. What have you been doing?"

"I had no idea it was going to be like this. I don't even know where to begin. I've been all over and I haven't seen anyone…"

This seemed to make her feel a little better and I could tell that if I didn't have to leave, we'd be on our way to get coffee and bagels. There was nothing that I wanted more, except that now I was on Paul's clock. Now I was going to be late even though I had promised him I wouldn't be. He wasn't going to understand, just like she didn't understand. It was impossible for touring to keep going on the way it was. There was never enough time in the day to juggle it all.

"Will I see you tonight?" She stared at the flat mattress and zipped up carry-on behind me. "Will I see you today at all?"

I almost told her yes, so that I could buy time, so that I could leave right this second and at least appease Paul. But it would be a lie. As it was, I was already driving up and down the state. I couldn't add anything more to this about-to-pop overinflated balloon.

"No. Today is even busier than the last two days. But I was asked to come back again. Maybe in May?"

"Ok." She closed her door and I stared at it, wishing she could understand what it was like to be in my shoes.

If anyone knew me, she did. My intentions were good, even if I had bitten off more than I could chew, but all I could think about was how I was digging the already present rift between us deeper. The one that had started years ago when I had joined the Air Force, when I was living in her basement, when everything was fun and fine until the day I decided I didn't want to owe her for the rest of my life. I left and never came back except to visit, and now I was living in a fantasy world, playing author.

Driving up to Paul's lot, I forgot all excuses when I saw his wife, the Santa Claus chairman from their *Ipods* charity and the Santa Claus chairman's wife all searching for something in Paul's SUV.

"How can ya lose ya wallet for Christ sakes?" his wife sighed.

"I think I found it," the Santa's wife said from the back seat. "It must have fallen out of his pocket."

"Mornin'," Paul said to me. "Get in."

When I was sandwiched between both wives, Santa's wife handed me a bottle of water and smiled.

"Thank you." I took a swig then pulled out my cell phone, put it in selfie mode, and started applying make-up.

"I didn't know the iphone had a mirror," Paul's wife said.

"It doesn't. I'm just using the camera as one. I've been trying to sleep 'til the latest minute possible and so I've been doing my make-up in the car every day."

"You workin' this girl to death, Paul?" his wife asked. Then to me, when he didn't answer: "Looks like you're really good at it."

Paul glanced at me in the rear view mirror like he was sorry and I shrugged back like it was okay. A few days ago I'd thought of him as a mafia guy, and now, like a Dad.

"You're the writer," Santa's wife said. "What do you write?"

"I wrote a memoir about my life in the Air Force."

"What made you do that?"

"I just felt like I had a story to tell."

"I can tell you some stories," Santa turned around from the front seat. "You wouldn't believe everything I see just from being Santa."

"You mean you don't just get a list of toys?"

"Are you kidding? I get all sorts of stuff."

"Tell her about the girl." his wife interrupted.

"Had this whack job asking me for her boyfriend back. Said she couldn't live without him and that's all she wanted for Christmas and that I had to promise to bring him back."

"What did you tell her?" I laughed.

"What could I tell her? I told her, yeah, of course I'll bring him back. And she made me promise over and over again and stood in line twice just to make sure I'd do it."

"What else?" I couldn't stop laughing until he said, "There was a boy one year who'd lost his father. That one was tough. The boy asked me to bring his father back, said the only thing he wanted for Christmas was to see his father again…"

"That's terrible. I never even considered things like that. What did you say? How could you not cry?"

"I didn't know what to say to him. All I could think of in such a short time was to tell him his Dad was already here, all around him, and that he would see him unwrapping his gifts. He thanked me and I had to do everything in my power not to cry right there. But I did later."

"Wow." I fought back tears.

"That's how I got started in all of this. I did a favor for a friend whose son was bedridden, had no friends, and couldn't leave the house, he was so sick. And just to see him light up like that, I was hooked. I do this every year..."

"You want a story for your books? Tragedy? I'll tell you a story." his wife interjected.

"You gotta listen to this." Santa agreed.

"The first week we were married, one of my sisters died from an aneurism. She had a newborn and we took her in. Can you imagine that? Get married and then, Boom! A week lata inherit a child? Then my other sister died in a house fire, trying to save her two kids. She was screaming at the window and a neighbor called the fire department, but then the kids ran back to their rooms- they say that's really common when kids are scared and in a house fire- and she went back to get them and they all died because they got trapped. That's how they found her, hovered over her kids. By the time I got there, the police wouldn't let me in because the house was going to fall apart and I said the hell you ain't, and I went through that whole house looking for something to remember her by. The only thing untouched was her wedding dress. Only one wooden board connected the closet to the rest of the house and I jumped over it to get the dress. I still have it."

There was nothing I could say besides, "Oh my God."

I glanced around the somber car. Everyone sat quietly, having already heard the stories.

"We've been through everything, haven't we?" She looked at Santa so lovingly I felt nothing but admiration for those two, and if my ex-husband had ever looked at me even once the way he looked back at her when he said, "Everything," I knew I'd have been the luckiest girl in the world.

"My other sister's son died in a hunting accident. And do you know how they found about that one? Her neighbor is a nurse, and when they wheeled him into the hospital she was sick to her stomach because she knew right away it was him. She had to step out and call my sister. My brother's son drowned…"

"There's more?" My mouth hung open. How much could a person take? How much did she think *I* could take? Is that what they thought my life as a writer was about, taking in every tragedy and turning it into a story?

"Yeah," she nodded. "The drowning was just awful. Both boys went down to the river to fish that day and the river was unusually high. Well, one of them got pulled in by the tide. He was only five but he was heavy, and when the nine-year-old tried to swim after him he couldn't reach him. His father came running and said, 'It should have been you instead.'"

"What did that do to him? How old is he now?"

"Thirty-seven? Thirty-eight? Drinks every day."

"I can imagine," I said. I would have too.

"My niece. This one happened so fast no one saw it coming. Christmas Eve, she was trying to hurry and wrap presents for her kids and wanted to go to the neighbor's where she'd hidden the gifts. Tells her daughter she'll be right back, then crosses the street and there's a loud boom. Hit by a drunk driver and the guy got off because his father was a judge."

"I don't know if I can hear anymore." I hoped that would make her stop, but she took in another breath of air and was only silenced when Paul said, "We're he'a."

"This better make more money than it did last year or I'm not ever doing it again," Santa's wife said.

"Not kidding. Paul, this is the last year I'm wrapping gifts if we don't do well. It ain't worth this," Paul's wife agreed.

"We'll see. We'll see. Get set up already. I want to introduce Jennifah to the manager at Barnes & Noble."

"I had tried to get into this store by myself," I said, following Paul. "Usually Barnes & Noble is only booked a few months in advance, but this one, forget it. It's like a year out."

"Now you're with me. And I did try to get you in here, but they said they couldn't get your books in time."

I wanted to book with her right here on the spot, but I knew I had to take a step back and simply thank her, tell her I'd get in touch with her or I was going to end up in the grave.

A small line had formed by the gift wrapping station outside the store. Santa handed out brochures and explained what the charity was all about while the wives cheerily wrapped. I took my place between the two wives, wrapped a few gifts until I noticed one of the photo albums from the charity's visits to Walter Reid Hospital. I couldn't help but smile with tears in my eyes as I flipped through the pages and saw the smiles on the faces of the veterans they'd gone to see. I was so proud to be a part of this, to be around such good people, and knew that if Paul did call me back, I'd be on the next plane over.

"We have to go," Paul said. "Last radio interview and school speech then we'll come back, wrap a few more, and head out to the veteran's home. This is the big leagues!"

"Okay," I agreed absentmindedly.

I had done radio interviews before, but the enormity of the building hit me as we parked in the garage in front of it in downtown Boston and walked in like rock stars. We got name tags and were escorted upstairs to record.

"You're a natural, no editing," the host said after we finished the segment about the charity, where to find us for the gift wrapping event and online to donate, as well as my book.

"Thank you. Radio I can do," I thought about how long I'd been talking to airplanes on the radio now, about fifteen years, which to me, was pretty much the same thing as any other radio. "TV, I get nervous. Stick a camera in my face and a smile is plastered on my face like I'm a mannequin." I glanced at Paul, who nodded, his eyes getting heavy. I hadn't even considered how tired he must be after toting me around all day.

"One hundred and sixty thousand listeners will hear this. I wish you all the best."

"Thank you for having us," Paul said.

We took turns shaking everyone's hand and then the intern escorted us out to take pictures of us with the *Ipods for Wounded Veterans* charity banner before we disappeared into the elevator.

"I loved that!"

"You were good," Paul said.

"Thanks to you for giving me pointers before."

"Well, we did it. I can't wait to take a break when you leave. I'm taking two months off."

"You deserve it."

"Ready for the hour drive for the other school?"

"Yeah," I smiled weakly, wishing I could close my eyes for just a few minutes, until I remembered that feeling this good wasn't going to last forever. I had to take it all in, every second of it. "I can't wait to see those kids."

...

Hours later, I sat in the foyer of the Veteran home, along with Paul and his wife and the Santa Clause chairman's wife, as Santa went into the bathroom to get ready. Feeling incredibly accomplished, I couldn't believe the final stop from the last three days was upon me. Soon I'd be on the flight home, back with my kids, back to my day job.

Santa came out a few minutes later, let his wife fix the belt and fluff the beard, as we marveled at his authenticity. He donned the hat. The setup was complete.

I said, giddy, "I need a picture with you Santa!"

The few visitors and staff also wanted a picture.

"Here, by the tree, Santa," one of the nurses said.

"Ready?" The director led us down the hall, excitedly. "We will be in the wing where most of the coherent soldiers are, where they would probably appreciate this visit the most."

An uneasy feeling crept over me as the word "coherent" sunk in. The eerie quiet and pungent smell of urine grew stronger with every breath. I thought I was the only one who smelled it until Santa's wife glanced back at me and wrinkled her nose. "It is not supposed to smell like this in here."

"Shameful," Paul's wife hissed back, but Paul and Santa plowed full steam ahead.

Paul handed me the Santa bell and when the director opened the door and we saw two rows of beds of men who looked older than time, it hit me that I could never in hell work in a place like this or volunteer to be Santa Claus without crying all day long.

I rang the bell so hard I thought my ear was going to explode and didn't stop until we reached the first bed. Santa shook the man's hand. The man grinned like a five-year-old on Christmas morning.

"What can Santa bring you this year?" Santa asked.

"Nothing, Santa," he smiled even wider.

"Wow, I am glad you're a happy man and have everything!"

"I do have everything, Santa, I do!"

"Thank you for your service young man," Santa said, shaking his hand.

The next man wasn't as lively. He was frighteningly skinny, even though all you could see was his head poking out from underneath some blankets.

"I'm cold, Santa," he almost whispered.

My heart almost stopped with the bell. The wives glanced at each other and tried to keep their composures as they laid out candy canes on the small nightstand and a few "Dear Soldier" letters. It was boiling hot already and he was covered in blankets. Was this how it looked like when someone was about to die?

"Get this man another blanket." Santa glanced around, but it was obvious the two nurses weren't going to get another blanket as they attended to several other residents. Then Santa patted his shoulder and said shakily, "We will get you another blanket, okay?"

"Thank you, Santa."

"You are a brave man, sir. Thank you for your service."

I rang the bell again and the wives quickly assembled their stacks while Paul handed them keychains and stickers to place on top of the letters.

"Ho, ho, ho, what can Santa bring you?"

"Nothing," the man said evenly.

"I see you have books, how about some books?" Santa pointed at his nightstand piled with books at least two feet tall.

"I'm fine, Santa."

Behind me, one of the nurses whispered, "It's a shame. His family is only an hour away and no one comes to visit him. He has three bronze stars."

That threw Santa over the edge. Tears formed in his eyes so fast I thought, please, please don't lose it now or I will. Somehow he managed,

"I was in the Army too, and I thank you for your service."

"Can I get you anything special for Christmas this year, young man?" Santa moved on to the next resident who was in a wheelchair with his legs raised.

"Nothing for me, Santa," the man said calmly.

"You have everything you need? Good to hear!"

"I just want to get out of here."

"You'll get out of here. Maybe someday," Santa smiled.

"My legs don't work, Santa. I haven't walked in forty-three years."

If I hadn't been stunned into place, I would have run out and I knew that we still had another wing to visit.

"You have no idea how much I appreciate all that you've done for our country," Santa's voice cracked and I didn't even know how he had said that much.

"Thank you, Santa," he mumbled.

Before we made it into the hall, I was already crying. I turned around and saw that everyone else was too. Sympathetically, the nurse looked at us and said, "You have no idea how much this means to our residents," then led us through the long corridor to get to the next hall. "So many of them don't get visitors."

"Three Bronze stars," Santa said, dazed. "Three! Do you know what that man went through?"

I shook my head, ashamed because I didn't even know what that meant. Had he been shot? Saved someone? Three people?

"There are producers from Hollywood in this building, engineers, you name it. We learn so much from them," the nurse said.

"And then their own families forget about them," Santa's wife sighed.

No one said another word, not until we entered the next bay and I rang the bell mechanically and stopped for Santa to take the lead. The wives assembled and Paul assisted, and I found it hard to breathe and wondered if I'd ever be the same again.

The heaviness hit me like a brick once we were back in the SUV, as an American flag dangled from a pole on the side of the building. I couldn't even imagine what those men and women had been through, and here they stayed, day in and day out.

"We gotta hurry to get your cah," Paul said as Santa loaded up the trunk with his suit. The wives quietly climbed in on either side of me in the back seat.

"I should be okay," I said, so dazed I almost didn't care if I missed the flight. "Paul, I just can't thank you enough for these last few days. This experience…"

"You were a troopah," he said, and although I couldn't remember what sleep felt like or how I was going to pull off what he did, said, "I hope to carry all of this forward. I hope to make you proud."

"You already do," he nodded. "You already do."

Columbus, Ohio   October 24, 2015

Ohio was nothing like I expected. I leaned forward in the cab, ecstatic when I saw the heart of the city, clean and quaint, the dark sky illuminated by the glowing red neon Dispatch Newspaper and Sheraton signs.

"What a cute city!" I nearly shouted.

"There's a lot to do here. Especially downtown. You picked a great location." My enthusiasm wore off on the driver.

"I think so, too," I said more to myself when he stopped in front of the inn. I paid him, took my carry-on inside, and felt the long day catching up to me.

"Water?" The concierge handed me a bottle of water.

"Two, please." I showed him my driver's license, signed something, and was grateful that he didn't hold me up any longer.

Flopping onto the bed after I washed my face and brushed my teeth, I couldn't believe how long today had been. There were no direct flights from Vegas to here, which left me with a ten hour travel window. Then, a few weeks before coming here, I had added Arizona at the last minute, but only because the Barnes & Noble there had squeezed me in for a signing and my friend and former neighbor had agreed to tote me around.

I hadn't seen her in three years. She moved away shortly after the SWAT team incident, when they stun-grenaded her house at three A.M. one morning and arrested everyone outside. When I didn't see her lined up on the curb amongst everyone else from the house, I thought her dead until she finally texted me the following day that she was out of town and had no idea what was going on.

For weeks I hounded her for details, but she said she didn't know anything. Then she came over one day, said everything she owned was bugged by the FBI because her sister had robbed a bank and they hadn't found the money. So I dubbed her "the Bank Robber's Sister" and had been plotting a book to write where I could name a character "the Bank Robber's Sister," ever since.

"The Bank Robber's Sister" took me to the most touristy restaurant in town, per request, then to Barnes & Noble where she said she couldn't wait to see me in action. However, it should have all been foreshadowing to me that morning when the airline insisted on checking my luggage and I then found out they had "mistakenly" forwarded it all the way through to Ohio and I was left without make-up or author clothes, and once we walked into Barnes & Noble, without my table and stacks of books.

The manager almost whimpered when she saw me, disappeared in the back, and came back in near tears, explaining she'd forgotten about me. All the additional money I had spent, the time I had wasted coordinating, and the hours I had lost with my children flashed before me as I demanded to know what I could have done better in all of this.

But all she said was, "Life happened." And I let it go because I had understood it completely. Life had happened to me too.

In the morning, I was up with the clouds and couldn't help but smile because my weather app had promised chance of rain for everywhere I had traveled to so far. I donned my usual of what I thought an author would wear: jeans, converse, blouse, blazer, and a long all-purpose scarf, and left my hair wet; who had time to fix pin-straight hair that wasn't going to hold anyway when there was a city to explore?

The GPS predicted an hour and a half walk and I still had three hours before my signing. I glanced in the full length mirror, ready to take on the world, and took a selfie. I looked professional, fun, and flipping cool, and I couldn't have been more amped as I stepped out of the elevator behind a woman who pushed herself ahead of me. I was living my dream.

Aimless at first, I took pictures of the skyline and the street, restaurants with interesting windows, a church with a stunning red door, beautiful flowers pots that lined the sidewalks that made this city so freaking cute, and then couldn't believe my luck when I discovered a huge stone statue of a man's head across the street. What kind of awesome company would have this in front of its building?

"Nice one!" someone yelled as I kissed the sandy cheek for a selfie.

"Thanks," I waved and wished random people would shout stuff to me like that back home.

A gust of wind tousled my hair and as if that was the push I needed, I was suddenly inspired. The air was so crisp. I breathed it in and the last few months, Seattle, flashed before me. I *could* write another book, about my adventures on book tour and all the people I'd met.

Luckily, I carried a notebook with me everywhere. I crouched down, slapped it on my knee, and jotted down ideas until I realized I didn't have time for this right now. I needed to get breakfast, take pictures, and take it all in!

"Excuse me, where is the nearest Starbucks? I figured there'd be one close, but I couldn't find it." I stopped a young man covered in tattoos and piercings carrying a cup.

"It's fucking right over there. Like, two fucking blocks down then fucking left." He replied so calmly I tried to picture what wonderful well-paying job he had that afforded him Starbucks and would let him talk like that.

I almost said, "Are you fucking sure, it's fucking right over there?" but managed a sweet, "Great! Thank you."

"Fuck, yeah." He brushed past me and I already knew when I turned the corner that I wasn't going to find Starbucks.

It didn't matter. I forgot all about Starbucks when I stumbled upon an Ohio-an Mecca, a long building wafting the smell of fresh bread towards me that said "North Market" on the side. Walking in, I was instantly transported back to Seattle's market. My eyes bounced from one local food stand to the next. I weaved through the busy aisles and felt overwhelmed until I saw Stauf's coffee, a no-brainer. That's where I'd start because when in Rome, one must drink the local coffee.

I took the first sip and time stood still.

"Can I buy this coffee by the pound to take home? This is literally the best cup of coffee I have ever had. I can remember the top five coffees I've had in the last ten years and this one wipes all of them clean off the board."

"Sure, right here," the barista chuckled. He walked me to the back. "This is the one I made for you."

I paid for it, shoved the pound of coffee into my bag, and asked the closest stranger to take a picture of me in front of Stauf's, so unbelievably satisfied that I had taken this trip to Ohio.

I finished my stroll with plenty of pictures and plenty of time to spare once I arrived at the college campus Barnes & Noble. I requested the manager, then walked around and looked at all the college humor t-shirts and gadgets until I heard, "I'm Martha. You're a little early."

"Hi Martha. I'm Jen. I was just walking around downtown and I didn't want to be late. Have you ever had Stauf's coffee? It's just amazing."

"It is." She softened a little and admitted, "This weekend has been hectic. The Buckeyes win a game and everyone sleeps in front of the store wanting a shirt the next day. This Barnes & Noble has the largest variety of merchandise and I'm just ready to retire, I guess. I've already been putting it off for two years."

"I saw when I was waiting. It made me want to buy one of everything." Except that the t-shirts had forty dollar price tags.

"Well, here we are," she led me to my table and I sat down feeling right at home as she excused herself.

Seconds later, a group of young girls came screeching at me then past me to the book stand right next to me, which held all the latest releases and best-sellers.

"Hi!" I said.

"Tyler Oakley!" one of the girls squealed, then all of them squealed and nearly pushed my table out of the way. "Here's a signed copy! Oh my God, he signed it. He was here yesterday and we missed it!"

"Who is Tyler Oakley?" I asked a mom as she sauntered up.

"Some guy on YouTube," she sighed, making me grateful that my kids weren't old enough for that yet.

I turned to see what the girls were looking at and stared at the cover of a man squinting, wondering what he had that I didn't, until I heard, "Is this you?"

"Yes," I smiled at the woman sadly admiring my book.

"You were over there?"

"I was. For six months."

"I'd love a copy. My son was there and he won't talk about it."

"My book isn't anything like that. I didn't see combat or anything. It's just about my experiences."

"I still want to read it. I want to know everything I can."

It looked like she was about to cry so I stood up and hugged her.

"Thank you," she sniffled, and I signed it for her, hoping it would give her the answers she wanted.

"Please look me up online if you ever want to ask me anything, okay?"

"I will."

And then I sat and watched the door, watched the clouds as they rolled in, watched as people watched me or fled past me to that book stand and made my peace with the fact that if I had made a difference in that mom's life, the whole trip had been worth it.

"You sold a few. That's good," Martha said. "It sure got dark out there fast."

"Is there a bus I can take? I don't feel like walking back in this."

"Yes, of course, I'll show you in a minute." She tidied up the books on the table then walked me towards the Military History section and asked, "What section do you want your book in. Barnes & Noble is changing some of their genres. Does Military History sound good?"

"I'd prefer Biography since it's really just the story of my life, part of which happened to be in the military." I tried to justify my cover that I sometimes felt was misleading, because it wasn't about the military at all, me, merely a player, just playing along, and the graininess of the photograph, representing the past, and how innocently I smiled, I thought, summed me up.

"Whatever you pick is fine with me," she said, then walked with me to the table. "Please sign the rest of them before you leave, though. I'll leave the table set up for a few days and then move them. When you're ready to leave, you'll walk up High St. and you should see a bus stop in about a block."

"Thank you for everything, Martha. I hope you have a great retirement." I waved and was out the door, happy that the rest of the night and the rain drops were mine.

Like Martha said, the bus stop wasn't far, and although I was happy enough to skip, everyone stood still and solemnly as they waited for his or her bus number, I couldn't help but wonder what was on their minds after a long work day as they let the misty rain slowly dampen their hair and faces.

"Can I take this bus all the way to the Book Loft?" I asked as I hopped on the first bus that said *German Village*.

"I'm not sure. I'll take you as far as I can, but you'll definitely have to switch buses and then from there you'll have to ask. I don't usually drive this route."

"Ok." I paid for the ticket and was about to sit in my own row behind a thin man I recognized leaning against the light pole at the bus stop until he said, "I overheard your conversation. I'm heading around there. I can help you get to where you're going."

"I'm okay. Thank you, though. It's not a big deal, I'm sure I'll find it."

He adjusted his baseball cap and I got a good view of his small eyes and way too skinny jawline.

"Are you sure?"

"Okay, why not?" I said, and moved up to sit next to him because I was on book tour after all and I was in need of adventure and most certainly couldn't turn down a good Samaritan. "Did you just get off work?"

"Yeah."

"What do you do?"

"I move furniture. It's not really what I do, but I needed something in the meantime and it's killing me."

"Oh. I can imagine," I said, thinking how much it must suck to lift people's heavy stuff all day.

"And you? What are you doing in Columbus? You're obviously not from around here."

"I'm an air traffic controller turned author on book tour. I happened to Google the top ten cities for book sales and Columbus came up. Barnes & Noble agreed to have me, so here I am."

"Author on book tour, huh?" he said pensively. "By yourself?"

"Yeah." I paused, knowing I'd divulged a little too much, but I was never going to see him again so what did it matter? "I got divorced about six, seven months ago now and I had to find a way to get out of the house and stop crying."

"Well, I tell you, that just sounds refreshing." He shook his head again, making me wonder what kind of people he knew if my sob story sounded refreshing.

"You're married?" I looked at his wedding band.

"Yeah."

"I'm Jen, by the way."

"Mark," he smiled. "Second wife. We're having problems. She's using drugs again. We've both been clean for years and now she's back at it worse than before."

"Does she work?"

"That's part of the problem. Her parents are well off. They live about an hour away and she was going back and forth for a while. And, it's just a mess."

Sometimes I wondered what people thought the real world was like. One had to pay bills and to pay bills one had to work. My Dad taught me that at age eight.

"How did you meet?"

"A few years ago I was living in Kentucky, working in the coal mines."

"How was that? Were you covered in dirt all the time?"

"Hard. Yeah, my hands. I could never get them clean. I hated it, but there's nothing else to do there, so you kind of have to."

"Did you dig?"

"No. I was the first guy in. I'd check to see if the opening was wide enough and then I'd set up the explosives."

"Was that scary?"

"Hell yeah. And it's hard to breathe and the hours are long and that's why everyone uses drugs, to stay awake and make more money, which is what I was doing. Then I never saw my wife and she was cheating but I couldn't do anything about it and I started cheating and realized too late that it was with my boss's wife."

"How'd you figure that out?"

"I saw his truck in the driveway one day and thought, hey I know that truck, and then I asked her. Then he figured it out and one day when I was down in the mines, something fell on my back and I couldn't walk. I filed Workers' comp. so he had me drug tested because he already knew I was using…"

"What were you on?"

"Meth. Almost everyone does meth or whatever you can get your hands on. And then I got fired and my wife had been sleeping with one of my friends, so I gave her the house for our two-year-old son and I moved back here...And, oh, your stop is coming up next. You'll take the bus that takes you to the end of German Village, okay?"

"Great, thank you." I stood up, disappointed our time was up.

"Sometimes real life is stranger than fiction," he smiled, and I said, "Yeah," wishing I knew what he meant, except that the door opened and I had to go.

From the curb, I turned around and waved as he waited for the doors to close, but before they did, he jumped out and said, "What the hell, I'll bring you."

"Don't you have to go home?"

"It's not every day I meet an author. I like your story. I'll take you."

"Thank you," I said, both a little nervous and excited at the same time. "Do you know where the Book Loft is?"

"It's not far at all," he said, and in minutes the bright red building was in sight.

"Yeah, that's it." I recognized it from the pictures on the Internet. "Have you been here before?"

"No." Mark shook his head and I understood that he was way out of place. He then followed me in.

"Pictures," I waved at him to lean in for a selfie with me.

"Not me," he said.

"Okay, then take one of me, please."

Then I turned around and felt overwhelmed by all the cluttered books. I had wanted to buy something, just so I could say I had bought something from here, but I drew a blank. Thankfully, the man behind the counter said, "More upstairs folks!"

"Thank you," Mark said, obviously uncomfortable.

"I won't be long. This is a bit much, even for me."

"Are you sure?"

"Yup. I don't even know where to start. This is a maze and I don't need more weight in my carry-on. The pictures are good. Let's get something to eat."

"Eat?"

"Aren't you hungry? Or do you need to get home? I forgot you had to get home."

"No, I don't. Where do you want to eat?"

"First place we see," I said, back on the street. "I can't believe it's still raining."

"It rains a lot here."

"Stauf's! Oh my God, have you ever had their coffee? I just had it today and it was amazing. See, I bought a pound of it and I think the guy mentioned they were building another location in German Village and here it is."

"No coffee for me," he said, shoving his hands in his coat pockets.

"You don't know what you're missing. What do you think of that restaurant? G. Michael Bistro? That looks good."

"It looks expensive."

"I'll buy."

"I won't eat."

"Stop it. This is an adventure. You have to eat."

Mark opened the door and it was glaringly obvious that he would never be caught dead in there. The host wouldn't look at him and neither would the waiter, which infuriated me, and as we sat down I made it a point to only stare at Mark and make him feel like he mattered. I asked, "What are you in the mood for?"

"I'll just have a beer," he glanced up.

"Water, no ice, for me."

The waiter rambled off the specials. Mark squirmed.

"We just need a minute," I said.

"It's a little pricey, isn't it? Oh, but you get a write off, right?"

"I don't. But please. I'm hungry and I'm sure you are, or did your wife cook? Will she know you were out? Are you going to get in trouble?"

"Her? Cook?" he laughed to himself. "Yeah, I'm going to get into trouble. But why not? Maybe the lasagna looks good. I'm only having a beer though."

"Then I'll order for you," I said, and told the waiter, "Lasagna for him and the tofu and eggplant and a starter salad for me."

"Do you have a prescription?" Mark studied me as he tried his beer, drinking from the bottle and purposely ignoring the glass. "To deal with everything?"

"You mean, do I take drugs?"

"Yeah."

"Never. Percocet once when my wisdom teeth were removed and then after my C-section because I couldn't walk. But I was miserable the whole time. When the divorce happened, I started drinking wine to relax and fall asleep, but a quarter or a glass knocked me out and then I felt like crap the next day. So I drank about two bottles in six months and thought, that's enough."

"Your ex-husband is an idiot. I can barely even look at you. You're beautiful, you know."

"Thank you."

"And easy to talk to."

"How's your beer?"

"Great. It's been a really great evening. I can't ever repay you."

"You just did. I'm glad I met you and you came with me. I don't want to pry, but will you tell me what you meant earlier when you said 'life is stranger than fiction'?"

"My life. This, right now, is just incredible, meeting you like this, and I have a story, but I don't know if you'd believe me, but I feel like I can tell you anything so what the hell. Where do I start? Growing up, my mother didn't come home one day…"

"What do you mean? How old were you? What happened?"

"She went to the store and never came back."

"Never came back? Were you devastated?"

"Of course. I was only nine. She was murdered."

"Murdered? They told you that?"

"I didn't find out until later. When I was eighteen and the Social Security checks stopped coming and I started doing some research. I lost my mom one year and then my dad the next. They never found her body, but her brothers thought my dad did it, that he had found about an affair, so they lured him into the woods and killed him. Made it look like an accident. I started drinking when I found out."

I would have too.

"Do you have siblings?"

"I have one sister, but she ran away after my dad died and I haven't seen her since."

"I can't even imagine growing up like that."

"What can you do?" he shrugged. "This lasagna is pretty good. How's yours?"

"It's okay. I try to eat healthy when I'm traveling. I think you should take it home and I hope you don't get into trouble."

"I'll explain I met an author who bought me dinner," he laughed. "No one would believe that story."

"No one would believe your story," I said.

He ordered another beer and said, "You inspired me today."

"I did?"

"Yup, you did. Can I come visit you in Las Vegas? I've never been there. Maybe I can find a job and start over like you did."

"Well, yes, of course you can visit. But it's a hard town to get used to. Are you sure that's what you want to do?"

"I am." He nodded, took a long and final swig from his beer and I wondered how much of his plan was truth or daydream.

"You can start over anywhere. It doesn't have to be in Vegas."

He didn't hear me. His eyes were far away.

"I'm going to read your book and then I'm going to find you online and I'm going to start over. I'm going to be a better person from now on."

"I hope you do and I'll help you however I can."

"Good."

"Are you taking the leftovers?"

"Nah, I shouldn't."

"Take them home to your wife."

"She'd love it."

"She'd never believe what happened tonight."

"You're right. Just toss 'em."

Nashua, New Hampshire   September 26, 2015

Nothing like being back in New Hampshire, I thought as I pulled up my chair, sipped my coffee, and took in the aroma of books that I'd come to know and love. Every Barnes & Noble smelled the same and every Barnes & Noble made me want to go through every aisle and touch all the books to see what I could find. Watching people as they came through the door in hopes of finding something was just as rewarding.

"Can you help me find a magazine?" a middle-aged man approached me.

"Sure, they're over here. Which one?" I took him over to the magazine wall.

"The one with Caitlyn Jenner."

"I think it's sold out, otherwise I'm sure it would pop out at us. Maybe you can ask at the front desk to reserve one for you?"

"Thanks, I will."

I went back to my table and noticed how many kids were in the store. In all the New Hampshire stores I noticed a lot of kids, which made me happy.

"Hi," a young boy said as he snuck up to the side of my table.

"Hi!" I said back, but he scurried away.

Then I noticed a young man staring at me from a chair. When our eyes met, he quickly covered his face with a book as if he'd been reading it all along.

"Do you mind signing this for him?" A woman suddenly blocked my view, the boy from a few minutes ago by her side. "He wanted to meet you, but he's a little shy."

"I would love to." I stood and shook his hand. "What's your name?"

"Adam," he whispered.

"I'm Jen," I said, and signed a book and handed it to him. "You are my youngest fan. What do you think about that?"

Adam smiled and as I turned to warn his mom about the language in it, her smile was even bigger than his and I didn't want to spoil the moment. I was sure she'd go through it first anyway.

"Want to take a picture with me, Adam?"

"Really?"

"Sure! Mom, do you mind?"

"Thank you for this."

"Thank you," I smiled and waved back at Adam, who turned around several times before he finally made it out the door.

Then I noticed a young man in a chair in one of the aisles. He covered his face with a magazine as soon as our eyes met. It was obvious he'd been eavesdropping and I wondered if I knew him.

"You're an author?" A ghostly looking man with white wispy hair and missing teeth stepped in front of me.

"Yes, hi! I'm Jen. This is my book. I wrote a memoir."

"Do you know when Harper Lee's new book *Go Set a Watchman* will be out?"

It was hard not to stare at the holes in his faded white t-shirt, at his pajama pants and coffee cup, as if he'd just decided to roll out of bed and get coffee at the bookstore and see who he could strike up a conversation with.

"Any day now, I think." I glanced at the poster behind him, boldly advertising when *Go Set a Watchman* was due to be out. That poster haunted me every signing I went to. Hell, it was already announced as the biggest selling book on Amazon ever and it wasn't even out yet, and I wished I could get even a measly one one-thousandth of that kind of publicity.

"I bet it's going to be good," he said.

"Yeah, I've heard several different reviews on NPR…"

"Reviews? Harper Lee is an icon, a classic, a writer of real American history! Do you know how long I've waited for this? I can't believe I get to see it in this lifetime."

"Well, there are lots of great-"

"Nonsense. There's a reason every school in America reads that book."

I didn't have the heart to tell him I didn't remember anything at all about *To Kill a Mockingbird*, only the black and white movie from class and only because I had read some trivia about the movie and found out that it made Robert Duvall famous. Of that movie, really, the only thing I recalled was Robert Duval wedged behind a door because the look on his face was so weird.

"Have you ever read Capote? I was floored when I found out Dill was Truman Capote. I mean, to go from *Breakfast at Tiffany's* to *In Cold Blood*, I was fascinated, and his style. So effortless, like Hemingway and their feud…"

"Hemingway is untouchable."

"He *is* untouchable. How about any other classics?"

"There is nothing better than the classics."

"That's what I used to think because I loved watching Jeopardy and being able to answer questions, but then I read *Gone with the Wind* and didn't think it was a love story at all, even though that's what the cover said. And *Moby Dick* four or five hundred pages about the specifics of tying knots."

"They're classics," he shook his head. "You can't mess with the classics."

"Victor Hugo?"

"Never got into him."

"Really? *Les Mis* is my favorite book of all time. It's a-mazing."

"They're all great, but can you imagine this treasure? They found this manuscript on her shelf. It's remarkable."

"Did you read *The Mockingbird Next Door*? It was written by a journalist and is about her experiences with Harper Lee. It wasn't as good as I thought it was going to be, but it was interesting."

"Nah, I've been dying for another actual Harper Lee book. What does some journalist know?"

"Yeah, that's what I thought when I was reading it."

"I went down there several times to see her."

"In Alabama? I only know because I just read that book."

"Yes. I went several times to Monroeville and never had the chance to see her. You should go. You wouldn't believe all the history there."

"Maybe someday. The book tour has been taking up a lot of my time, but I do have *Go Set a Watchman* on my book list. I was going to wait a while to read it, but you're definitely getting me all hyped up about it."

"Hyped up? I haven't been able to sleep for weeks. I'm planning another trip down there. I used to go with a few friends but they're dying off. You should definitely look into going."

"I have two young kids. It wouldn't be possible right now and to be honest with you, I barely remember to *Kill a Mockingbird*. I'd have to reread it. *Go Set a Watchman* is supposedly a continuation of *Mockingbird*, right?"

"I don't care what it is. She can't do no wrong."

"Well. Hard for me to compare anything to that."

"I wish you luck."

"Thanks," I said and he left, my view on the chair again, making me wonder if I knew this guy, which I didn't think I did. If he was eavesdropping, why didn't he just say hello?

All of a sudden Pat, from the flight in appeared.

"Pat? You made it!"

"I told all my friends about you and I can't wait to read it. Will you sign it for me?"

"Of course I will. How are your mom and friends? Have you done everything you wanted to do?"

"Everything is great. My mom's hanging in there and yeah, I'm pacing myself. Have you heard from Crystal?"

"I texted her a few times, but I don't think I'll see her because I fly back on Monday."

"Me too. Ten A.M.?"

"Ten A.M.," I nodded. "This world is so small."

I noticed the guy in the corner was still staring at me and made up my mind to talk to him as soon as I could because he obviously wanted to talk to me.

"I guess we'll be sitting together then too, ha! I won't keep you. I know you have lots of people to talk to."

"Thanks for coming! I'll see you Monday."

As Pat left, I started walking towards the guy in the chair, only to find that he had vanished into thin air, making me wonder if I'd made him up. Slowly, I made my way back to my table and realized that I was going to have to accept all the things that came at me, especially things out of the ordinary, whether it was on book tour or in real life.

That was the new me. Learning how to roll with it.

Then I remembered Joe from the mall and how there was no way he was going to show up now since it was almost time to leave. And to think I had gotten excited about him coming back. Oh well. One of these days, it was going to happen. It had to. A guy wasn't going to be intimidated by me and we were going to have the best time of our lives, even if I never saw him again.

Burlington, New Hampshire September 27, 2015

Coming off the highway exit, the Barnes & Noble was the biggest I had seen so far. Once I stepped inside, I still couldn't get over how massive it was and nearly bumped into my childhood friend, who'd been standing by my table waiting for me.

"Lourdes!" I hugged her. "Thank you so much for coming! And thank you for your friend who helped me with the edits. I wouldn't have been able to do it without her."

"Oh, no problem," Lourdes smiled shyly. She hadn't changed at all since eighth grade and I was glad when I got the chance to see her when I flew into town.

"You're going to sign my copy, right?" She pulled my book from her purse while I whipped out my Sharpie.

"Great to see you getting started already," the manager approached me. "I'm Sue and I'll be doing a few announcements for you starting in a few minutes if that's okay? Do you want me to introduce you as Jennifer or JG?"

"Thank you, Sue. Either one is fine," I said, and she left to make the announcement, which made Lourdes almost jump up and down with excitement.

"I'm so excited for you," Lourdes said.

"Thank you. Really. How's everything with you? Are you still liking Raytheon?"

"I can't complain. I actually love what I do, but sometimes I find that I can't pull myself away from my desk."

"Hey, can I ask you something?" a man with a briefcase interrupted us.

"Ask away," I said, feeling like we were having a water cooler meeting.

"How did you get published? I have all these manuscripts in my drawer. I'm always writing, but I don't think it's worth publishing."

"What good are they doing in your drawer? Mine sat in a drawer too. I hired an editor who told me I didn't know how to write and then she helped me at least get started. Every time I gave up, I went back to it thinking I have a story to tell. And so once I finished my draft, I started researching publishers and agents and query letters. What's the harm in contacting a publisher?"

"I write for a living and I do pretty well at that, so it seems like a waste of time."

"What do you write?"

"Manuals mostly. I do technical writing, but I've dabbled in stories."

"I think you should give it a try, why not?"

"Okay, I guess you're right." He walked away as if he was blowing me off.

"I'm serious," I followed him. "It won't take up that much of your time since you already have them finished. Most authors write about three or four books before they find a publisher. I got denied a lot, but each time I learned something more and I built upon that and then tried again and again. I think you should give it a go and you can always look me up if you have more questions."

"I guess you're right. I'll think about it," he said unconvincingly and left.

"It's the number one question I get, Lourdes, and I can't understand why people give up. Every time I gave up, I pulled it back out and said 'nope, I have a story to tell' and I would rewrite and submit because I knew that really, all I needed was one person to like me."

"Not everyone is you, Jen."

"Aw. Lourdes."

"You should be proud of all you've accomplished, Jen, especially given what you've been through."

"Thank you for being my friend all these years."

"That's what friends are for," she said. "I'm going to get some coffee and let you get to work. Is there anything I can get you?"

"No. Thank you. I'll get one in a minute. Thanks again for coming. Let's take a selfie."

"Definitely."

"We'll grab lunch after if you want to stick around. I'll have about thirty minutes to kill before my next one."

"Okay."

Lourdes walked towards the café and as soon as I was seated I studied the door, my favorite activity in the world, waiting for the next adventure to unfold. Two men walked in, one short with broad shoulders and the other a lumber jack-looking man with a thick gray-brown beard and glasses whose shirt caught my eye: "Irony. The opposite of wrinkly."

I couldn't let him walk past me without commenting and said, "Excuse me, but I love your shirt. I just had to tell you that."

"Oh, which one am I wearing?" He looked down. "I have so many like this one. It's a good one, huh? I like it too."

"There're more?"

"Lots more. You're an author?"

"I am. It's a book about my experiences in the Air Force. How I joined, why I joined…"

"Okay," he shrugged. "Will you sign it for me?"

"I'd love to."

A second later, a woman walked through the door and instantly made a beeline for my table and said, "Alright, what are you selling?"

"It's my memoir. How and why I joined the Air Force."

"Why not? Can you sign it for me?"

"I would love to."

"Can't wait to read it." She patted the cover and was gone.

Through the door, the broad shouldered man from earlier came back in. I glanced at my watch and saw that it had already been an hour and waved at him. "Hi! You're back."

"Yeah. You noticed?" he said shyly.

"It's kind of what I do. I say hi to everyone."

"You're an author?"

"I am."

"That's you on the cover?"

"Yes. It's an older picture or me and grainy, but that was the idea. To make it seem distant and a long time ago."

"You know, I had a feeling about you."

"You did?"

"Yeah. What are the odds that you would recognize me and here we are talking?"

I didn't dare tell him that me saying hello to everyone was kind of the point. I was a glorified greeter hoping to sell my book to strangers.

"Do you mind if I sit down?" His gaze was distant, daydreamy.

"Of course not." I stood up to offer him my chair, but he pointed at a chair next to the table and sat down.

"I didn't even know that was there, huh."

"It feels so good to sit. My knees hurt. My feet hurt."

"I'm sorry to hear that."

He closed his eyes and rubbed his knees while I peeked up at the clock. I didn't have much time left and decided he would probably be my last sale. Then I was going to be off to have lunch with Lourdes and then go to my last signing of the day.

"Can I read your aura?" He opened his eyes and looked at me.

"I guess so."

"That's what I do. I heal through the aura."

He stood up as though his knees weren't bothering him at all, positioned himself right in front of me as I got out of my chair too, held on to my hand, and said, "Close your eyes. What color is your heart?"

"Oh, I thought you were kidding," I said.

"Close your eyes, dear. Tell me what you see. What color is your heart?"

"I have no clue."

"Yes, you do. Close your eyes and see, I mean really see. What is the color of your heart?"

"Purple?"

"Great. What is the color of my heart?"

"I don't think I'm any good…"

"Just tell me!"

"Red?"

"Yes, yes! See, isn't this marvelous?"

"I really need to go to the bathroom. I wasn't expecting-"

"Our hearts together? What do you see?"

"Yellow?"

"Yes, yes," he paused. I opened my eyes slightly and watched him smile to himself. He was having so much fun I hoped he wouldn't figure out that I was just rambling off colors of the rainbow.

"Are you in pain?"

"No. What kind of pain? Should I be in pain right now?"

"Are you hurt?"

"Like what?" I asked. Could he see my divorced, broken, purple heart? Should I come clean? I shook my head blindly. "Not that I know of."

"Hm. Shoulder issues? I'm showing you have a bad shoulder."

"Well, I work out. I lift weights, is that what you mean?"

"No, that is not what I mean. The reading is very strong. I know your shoulder hurts."

"Okay," I agreed, thinking maybe he'd misdiagnosed the area since my bladder was howling.

"How about your arm?"

"No."

"Your elbow?"

"No," I said, and opened my eyes to get an idea of what the hell he was doing and saw that his cheeks were flushed with embarrassment. What could I possibly say?

"What is the color you feel all around you?"

"Blue?"

"You're a natural. You're amazing. I was sent here to heal you, do you believe that?"

"Yes," I said, hoping this would speed up the process so I could run to the bathroom. I cursed myself for drinking so much coffee and water.

"Do you feel my color all around you?"

"Yes, yes. I do. It's green."

"I knew there was something about you. How do you feel? You can open your eyes now."

"Great, thank you."

"Here's my card. Look me up when you're back in town and we can make some progress."

"I will!"

"You'd better. I'll be waiting for your call."

"I'll call!" I said, and flashed my best smile.

But what the hell had just happened?

Salem, New Hampshire   November 8, 2015

"I'm JG, the author. I'm sorry I'm late," I said as I approached the woman behind the counter.

"Don't be silly," she smiled. "Welcome, I'm Sharon, and you're right on time. Please make yourself comfortable. Here's your table. We have our charity group here, *Ipods for Wounded Veterans*, and all sorts of workshops set up over there. It's been nuts all day and the day isn't even close to being over yet. We're trying to beat what we pulled in last year. Here's a stack of paper and pens if anyone wants to write any "Dear Soldier." Letters and the mailbox for it is upstairs."

"What a great idea." I smiled at one of the sample letters. When I was overseas I had received some and had loved them.

"I love this charity," Sharon gushed. "I've been working with them for years and it's amazing what they do. Oh, I'm needed. Settle in, get a coffee or a sandwich from the café, anything you want off the menu, okay?"

"Thank you so much, really. Wait, where's Mel? He was really great last time and he was the one who invited me back."

"He's pursuing other opportunities," she said with finality, and I hoped it didn't mean he'd been fired.

In the café, I ordered my usual iced mocha and a pizza, fascinated that pizza was even a feature at Starbucks and/or Barnes & Noble. Once I had eaten, I strolled over to the workshop tables that I had originally thought would be for other authors when Mel had told me about them.

One workshop table was a local carpenter shop that printed 3D designs. I couldn't resist inspecting all of the robots and gadgets. I observed the printer at work before I noticed a man with a backpack standing there with a remote. Attached to the backpack was a thick plastic straw that held a color changing cotton cloud stationary above him.

"That is so cool," I said.

"It's my cloud." He showed me the Cloud app on his phone. It contained a menu of different colors. He asked, "Get it?"

"I do. It's very clever. Can we do a selfie?"

"Here, change the color and then we'll do a selfie," he said. "Cheese."

"What's this?" I moved to the next table and was fascinated by a small knitted cactus and tree that looked like Groot from *Guardians of the Galaxy.* "Did you knit these?"

"I did."

"They're amazing. And Groot looks so real."

"It's so easy," the woman said. "You can come to my workshop. It's free and you'll make your own in a few hours."

"I wish, but I live in Vegas. I'm an author and have my table set up over there. I'm just kind of wandering around."

"Oh. Well, maybe if you come back and you're in town for longer?"

"Definitely."

"I'll come check out your book later."

"Ok, great! But first, you have to take a picture with me."

Back at the table, a young guy was looking at my book and asked shyly, "Is that you on the cover?"

"Yes," I smiled.

"I'm Mike, one of the volunteers here for the charity and-"

Suddenly, I saw Ozzie, my partner in crime in basic training, in front of me and I couldn't help myself but scream, "Ozzie!"

"I drove two hours to see you!"

"Mike, I'm so sorry…"

"No, no, I'll catch you later."

"Ozzie! You came for me!"

"I can't believe you still call me that!"

"That's your name, what else would I call you?"

"Cheryl?"

"I will try to call you that, Ozzie, but I don't know if I can. I'm so glad you drove up here. It's been what? Seven years?"

"About that. I tried to make it last time, but my sister was getting married and I couldn't do it."

"I'm happy to see you whenever. Is this your daughter?" I kneeled to get a better view of her two-year-old, but she had no interest in me and walked in circles around the table instead. "I've only seen her on Facebook. She's beautiful!"

"I was hoping to meet your kids," she smiled. "They're plastered everywhere on Facebook."

"Everyone at my work says if they're ever kidnapped they won't get far since everyone knows what they look like. I had to leave them at home with the ex, though. It's just too much to take them with me on signings because I try to be in and out as fast as I can."

"I'm sorry about all that," she said.

"It's okay. When I see your pictures of you and your husband, they make me happy and it gives me hope that there're great guys out there."

"First one, yuck, you remember. This one is a keeper. It will happen for you, too. Oh, before I forget, let me show you…" She pulled out our yearbook from basic training and found the page where I'd signed, *Ozzie, I never would have made it through basic without you! Let's stay in touch!* "And we did, didn't we?"

"It's true. I never would have made it without you."

"I loved how you made fun of the drill sergeant behind his back. *Air-man!* That was so funny."

"I actually think you were funnier than me. I was dying most of the time and you were like, yeah, I love getting dirty and doing pushups and spit shining…"

"Shut up," she pushed my shoulder playfully.

"No, it was great. I thought you were nuts. And you still love it."

"I do."

A woman picked up my book and I waved my hand in front of Ozzie and said, "If you read the book, this is Ozzie," and Ozzie cracked up. The woman smiled and said, "You were in the military? You're too beautiful to have been in the military."

"Go on," I laughed.

"I'm being serious."

"Thank you," I said thinking this was exactly why I kept coming back to New Hampshire.

"Ok, I'll take one."

"Fantastic," I said.

"You won't be disappointed," Ozzie said as I signed it. "That's it for me, Jen. I have to get her home."

"I'm so glad you came to see me, Ozzie."

"Me too."

Although I wanted to make another round at the craft tables, Pam's dad, Mr. B. walked in.

"Hey, Mr. B! Did you come here for me? You came to my very first signing already!"

"Of course I came. I had to see the famous author."

"Ha, ha."

"Remember the book you signed for my friend? He says he doesn't want to read it. He insists it won't interest him."

"That's fine. I'm sure there are people out there who don't like it."

"It's a great book. How can I get him to read it?"

"Maybe he will read it eventually. You want me to talk to him?"

"Yeah. Let's do that. We can call him in the morning. He's always sitting at Dunkin Donuts. Maybe we'll even run into him."

"Thank you, Mr. B. I'm sure we can get him to read it. I'll see you later for pizza."

"Oh, hey, don't I know you?" I waved at a man with glasses. "You were the teacher. You come here all the time and I think you said you were writing a book too and that you couldn't afford my book the last time I saw you."

"Yes, I'm Jim. I remember you. Yeah, I come here all the time to work on my book. And

I'm sorry I still don't have the money to buy one of yours. They keep cutting my salary."

"I know, you told me that the last time. I don't care about that. Come here, let's take a picture."

"Okay," he sighed, reminding me of a neurotic Seinfeld character as he nervously shifted his glasses and put down his distressed leather briefcase.

"It was good to see you, Jim! Maybe I'll see you again if I come back!"

"That sounds great. I'm going to the café now to work on my book."

Coming off the escalator was Mike, the shy guy from earlier. He looked right at me and asked, "Hey, do you have a minute now?"

"Sure. Are you okay?"

"I was overseas too and I hadn't really thought about it in a while until I saw you and your book and well, I just never really talked about it before with anyone. Something made me want to talk to you."

"When I was overseas, the guy who was in charge of us told me that it takes years to talk about what happened. And it was true. I didn't talk about it with anyone. And then my dog died, a dog I'd gotten to help me feel normal again. When he was gone, I couldn't stop crying and I started writing and talking about what had happened. What did you do when you were there?"

"MP."

I nodded.

"I…"

I hugged him and he wouldn't let go.

"It's going to be okay, I promise. It might take a while. It took me four years just to feel normal again and it wasn't until the book was done that I thought, wow, this was just a story. Okay?"

"Okay." He finally pulled away.

"You can look me up anytime."

"Okay," he said and left.

"JG? I've been meaning to talk to you." A man approached me with his hand extended. "Mike is helping me out upstairs. I'm one of the board members for *Ipods for Wounded Veterans* and if you're interested in doing radio and TV, I can hook you up with Paul, who oversees all that. Would you be interested?"

"Definitely, thank you so much for thinking about me." I shook his hand. "I actually did a TV interview in Chelmsford yesterday. The more the merrier."

"Great, great. Here's my phone, it's already ringing. Just tell him who you are and hopefully you can work something out."

Las Vegas, Nevada   June 14, 2015

Up and down the aisle on the Southwest flight, only middle seats were available. I called it the businessman sandwich. Essentially, every seat was the same and I usually picked the first one so that I was one second faster getting out, but this time something told me to keep going. I was going to let the seat pick me.

This sounded stupid as I thought about it some more, and I nearly plopped down my carry-on in the next seat until I saw them. Two blonde women, mother and daughter, in row twenty-two with the middle seat open.

"Is this one taken?"

"Oh no." The mother got out of her seat and took my bag. "Let me help you with that."

"Thank you so much," I said, wanting to help, but she shoved the bag into the compartment like a pro.

"Sit down, sit down," she said sweetly. Her daughter moved back a few inches into the window although there was nowhere else to go and asked, "Do you have enough room? How are you?"

"Great now," I smiled at both of them. "I have flown so much and have always been in the middle seat, but it seems never with women. I had to sit with you."

"Welcome to the party. We just met too."

"Really? You look like mother and daughter!"

"That's what we were just saying. I'm Pat," the older one said, but really, she was a carbon copy of Meg Ryan.

"Crystal," the young one smiled, her long blonde hair flowing past her elbows.

"Jen," I said. "And both of you live in New Hampshire?"

"Oh, no," Pat waved. "I escaped over twenty years ago. I'm in Reno now."

"Me too," Crystal said. "The only flight to New Hampshire leaves through Las Vegas."

"Wow, what are the odds? I love flying into Manchester and Southwest used to offer a direct flight year round, but I found out they only do it in the summer now. It's my favorite airport in the whole world."

"Mine too," Pat said.

"It's so small and convenient," Crystal agreed.

"So then you're visiting family?"

"Yes, my mom and brothers are ok. When I first moved away for college, I ended up going to New Zealand to study..." Crystal said.

"What did you study? That seems so far away to go for college."

"It was just a program that they offered. It was for a course in archaeology and it was the most fantastic experience of my life."

"It sounds like it. Do they have gigantic spiders? I just heard that Australia has big ones that fly or leap from the trees. I just couldn't."

"There were a lot of spiders. But there is so much to do there. I would go back in a heartbeat."

"What about you, Pat?"

"I just felt like getting away," she shrugged. "It was so boring growing up. I wanted something different. I met my husband and we settled in Reno. I'll never leave there. It's just breathtaking; the mountains, right on the water, and the weather is perfect. I come back to New Hampshire to visit my mother and some friends and it's beautiful, don't get me wrong, but I'm so at home in Reno now."

"Me too," Crystal said.

"Yeah, I feel that way about Vegas now, too. I've actually never been to Reno. I don't know why. It's only a few hours from Vegas, right?"

"One hour," Pat said.

"And I heard it's beautiful, especially Tahoe, and I've said I'd like to go up there and I haven't."

"Well, then come up there," Crystal shrugged. "Are you going to see family in New Hampshire too?"

"I am. And, well, I got divorced recently."

"Oh no, I'm so sorry," Crystal said.

"It's okay. I'm okay now because of the traveling, really. I wrote a book and now I'm on book tour."

"How exciting!" Crystal said.

"Where are you signing?" Pat asked. "I'll try to go."

"Me too."

"I'll be in Nashua, Burlington, and Salem. I can text you the dates and times when we land and if you two can make it, then great."

"You two could really pass for sisters," Pat marveled.

"We could pass as family," Crystal said.

"Honestly, I feel like I've known both of you all my life. It's settled then. Let's plan to meet every year."

"You could do a signing in Reno," Pat suggested.

"I hadn't even thought of that, but yeah, I'll work it in. Great idea! Maybe around Thanksgiving?"

"Deal," Pat said.

"Deal, Sis," Crystal nodded.

Manchester, New Hampshire June 14, 2015

Lost in the Mall of New Hampshire, I could have sworn there was a Disney Store in there somewhere.

"Hey, I'm not stalking you or anything," a cute guy my age suddenly bumped into me.

"What did you say?"

"I was kind of close behind you because you slowed down, so I didn't want you to think I was stalking you."

"Ha," I laughed, unsure if he was hitting on me or being serious. "I didn't even see you."

"Well, I hope you see me now." He extended his hand. "Joe."

"Jen. Nice to meet you, even though you weren't stalking me. Sadly. Can you tell me where the Disney Store is?"

"God, they closed that, like, two years ago."

"That settles that then, I guess." I scratched my head, wondering what else I could get for the kids. "Thanks."

"What are you doing tonight?" he asked.

"Tonight?" I said, caught off guard and unable to remember the last time someone asked me out for a drink, or at all.

"Yeah, like later tonight, do you want to get a drink?"

"What time did you have in mind. I'm an author and I'm doing a signing today, in about an hour at Barnes & Noble down the street. If you want, you can talk to me there and…"

"At one o'clock?"

"Yes, until three."

"What did you write?"

"It's a memoir about my life in the Air Force, but I'm working on something else now, too."

"You were in the military?"

Regretting I'd told him the truth, he sized me up and I knew that look; me, a foot shorter than him, military. Author. No deal. Finally, I replied, "Yes."

"Oh, yeah, cool," he nodded and backed away. "I'll be there. We'll talk then."

"Bye." I waved, knowing it would be a miracle if he showed up. Then I GPS'd a Toys "R" Us, which was just down the street.

Standing at the register holding two Peppa Pig stuffed animals, I felt so proud of myself. I had talked the talk and walked the walk. I was tired, exhausted, and there was no break in sight, but I had done it.

Seven years it had taken me to finish my book and it all started because my dog Bishop had died. I say mine because I had rescued him from a shelter right after my deployment, when I was at my worst, still crying, having nightmares, and having a hard time even getting out of bed. Bishop changed my life until I met Sal.

I knew I'd marry Sal the second I saw him. Even now, I wanted to be so mad at him, to blame him for all of this, but the truth was, he, too, changed my life. We had accomplished everything we had set out to do and without us knowing it, we'd drifted apart.

When Bishop died and all the pain I hadn't dealt with from my time in the military came flooding back and I thought my life was over, I called a therapist because I couldn't stop crying and the receptionist laughed at me. It was then I decided to write. I just didn't realize it was going to be a book until seven months of writing had yielded so many pages that I knew I had to do something with it.

Publishers denied me and I researched how to become a better writer until I decided to hire an editor who loved my story but told me I didn't know how to write. She gave me writing assignments and pointed out the bad and some of the good until I said I could do it, I was going to do a rewrite and then contact her again.

A year later, she told me I had learned nothing. Everything was still the same. I wanted to rip my hair out because my first baby was due and I had wanted my book done. She told me to write as though I was talking to my unborn baby, and for some time it worked, until I realized that it didn't.

As fate would have it, my mother started dating an author, an eighty-something-year-old author who'd written horror and had shared the shelves with Stephen King. I loved all his books. He knew sarcastic dialog better than I'd ever read, and he agreed to take me under his wing. And so it began, me sitting across from him in his kitchen and my son sleeping in his swing while my mom tried not to laugh as he picked apart my writing.

It really was funny. It reminded me of watching someone learning to ride a bike and falling. Not that falling off of a bike was funny, but you knew what it felt like because everyone learning to ride a bike has fallen off and once you get it, there's no better feeling in the world. At night, he gave me homework. I read Henry Miller to learn about stream of consciousness, Hemingway for effortlessness, and Hunter S. Thompson for pace and tone.

By the end of another rewrite, I realized I had rewritten my book to sound as though an eighty-year-old man had written it. I rewrote it again. This time, I was armed with what I knew I wanted to say and it came out better than I had hoped. I loved every word. And now I was able to share it.

I thought about my kids as I held the stuffed animals close and wished I could give them a more normal life, one where I wasn't constantly working and one that wasn't split apart like this, half the week at Sal's and half with me.

It didn't matter that I planned all the tour dates while I was working. I still missed them. But this had to be done. I had to save myself, find myself again, and be the strong person that I was, stop crying in front of them and teach them how to be independent, like my mother had taught me growing up.

I thought of all the people who'd stopped by my table to say hello and had breathed life back in to me. How could I ever repay them for their time, their kindness, their generosity?

All I could do was hope I did the same for them, that I touched their lives in some way and that every day from here on out was going to be about me being a better me.

Salem, New Hampshire   June 14, 2015

"Anything you need from the café is yours," Mel said as he showed me to my table.

"Thank you, Mel," I smiled.

The first time I had spoken to him on the phone, my kids were on my lap screaming and I thought his name was Richard. I had emailed him the details of my book and he agreed to have me in his store for a signing, telling me that his name was Mel. I apologized that I had called him Richard and called him Mel in the next email, except that it autocorrected to smell and he again corrected me. His name was not Richard, or Smell, it was Mel. I died.

"I'll take an iced mocha, please."

"It's so good to be home," I sipped my coffee. "I love being here. This is my old stomping ground. I can't tell you how many magazines I would read here every week after school. Oh, I probably shouldn't be telling you that."

"Sell some books and I'll forget you mentioned it," he winked.

"I will." I admired my poster. I could get used to this.

"You went over there, huh?" An extremely handsome man picked up my book and admired my cover.

"Yeah, I went there. Some people said I divulged too much information, but what can I say?" I said stupidly, before I realized what he really meant. "I was deployed for six months. It was supposed to be a year..." I trailed off when his beautiful girlfriend walked up to him and put her head on his arm as if to claim him. She looked at my cover sadly and I wanted to tell her she had it all wrong. She was the one who had done everything right. I would have killed to be in her shoes with a guy like that, without having to have gone through all that I did to get here, because guys didn't know what to do with an independent girl like me.

"That's cool," he smiled weakly. "Actually, it's pretty amazing."

Then he put the book down, took his girl's hand, and walked away.

"Hi," I waved at a man. He glanced at my cover, pushed his glasses into his forehead and kept walking.

"Oh, I can't buy today." He switched his briefcase to the other hand nervously. "I'm a professor and they just cut my salary and…"

"It's okay, I was just saying hello."

"Hello," he managed. "I come here from time to time and I write. Sometimes I read the newspaper."

"I used to come here, too. I went to Salem High School."

"Okay. Okay," he nodded. "It was great to meet you. And, you know, good luck with the book. Are sales good?"

"Great."

"Good." He waved quickly, then seated himself in the café.

"Jean!"

"Jen!" Jean, my former boss from the hair salon I worked at before I joined, hugged me.

"I can't believe you came out here!"

"Are you kidding? I'll take two. One for my son and one for me."

"He's still in the Marines?"

"He is. And he's going overseas. I'm worried."

"Is he worried?"

"No. He can't wait."

"Then don't be worried. He'll be home before you know it."

"Dr. Lynne?" My chiropractor, whose daughter I'd gone to school with, showed up. Because of her regular adjustments, I credited her for making it possible for me to join the military without my inhaler. I didn't talk about it much because unless you've had regular adjustments, you simply wouldn't understand the amazing effects it has on your body.

"Hi, Jen," she hugged me. "Can you sign this?"

"You are seriously the only person I did not want to read this book." I opened the cover and signed it, my face red. "There's a lot of foul language, amongst other things."

"I haven't started it yet, but Charles is halfway through."

"And?"

"He loves it."

"Is he working at the hospital still?"

"Yes, a double shift today. Can you make it for breakfast in the morning?"

"I should be able to. How's Stef? I tried calling her, but she hasn't called me back yet."

Coincidentally, ironically, her daughter's husband had left her right after he finished his Master's degree, too. When it happened, I thought how horrible it was and that it would never happen to me. And yet here I was.

"Hey Jen!" My friend Rachel from high school stood in front of me with a smile. "I saw you were here and I couldn't make it last time, but I had to show up today to see you!"

"God, Rachel, I don't even know how long it's been since we've seen each other and gone roller skating."

"Tell me about it," she rolled her eyes. Roller skating had been her thing, everyone's thing back in the day, but while she won awards I could barely roll forward.

"Can I start reading your book now? Can you sign one and I'll, like, sit next to you and read?"

"You're going to be my groupie? Then that's how I'll sign the book. To my groupie, Rachel."

"You rock." She smiled to herself and started reading.

I looked up and saw a woman who looked familiar and said, "Hi."

"Hi," she looked at me, just as bewildered.

And then it clicked.

"Kathy, is that you?" She was one of Jean's hairstylists and I used to prank her all the time because she was so uptight. "Oh my God, what are you doing here? I almost didn't recognize you. I can't believe it's you. Jean was here about an hour ago and she said she lost touch with everyone, and here you are!"

"What am I doing here? What are you doing here? You wrote a book? Of course you wrote a book! Joins the military, writes a book. You're unbelievable, kid."

"And I just took pictures of you two recognizing each other." Rachel held up her cell phone, proud of herself.

"You're the best, Rachel. Kathy is in the book, I can't remember what page, but she was the best. I loved working with her. She would make me laugh so hard."

"Still a goofball." She looked at Rachel and pointed at me. "I'm in the book? Well then I'll have to get one."

"Thank you. Let me sign it. Is that your daughter? You remarried?"

"Yeah, it didn't work out with Mario." She frowned and I said, "Sorry," because I remembered him and I loved them together.

"I'm divorced now, too," I shrugged. "Two kids. Being divorced is definitely not how I saw myself."

"It will get better. I promise." She took my book and hugged me. "It was so good to see you. You're amazing."

"Rachel, what's up?" Pam came behind my table to hug Rachel.

"Hey, Pam, hi Mr. B.," I said to her father. It was starting to feel like Christmas with all the familiar faces. I couldn't remember the last time I felt so much love and support.

"Hey, Mr. B.," Rachel waved at Pam's dad, who'd taught at our high school.

"Hi, Rachel. Good to see you."

"Jen, I need a book for a friend. It's his birthday, if you don't mind signing it for him."

"I'm on it." I said, picking up a Sharpie.

I didn't see the woman in front of me until I heard Pam get excited and scream, "You have to read the book! My friend wrote it and I'm in it, we're all in it! It's so good!"

"Pam! Give her a minute!"

The woman dropped the book and hurried to the next table.

"Oops," Pam said, staring at me. "I love you Jenny."

"Love you, too. They will buy the book if they want to read it. Don't worry."

"I really do love it so far." Rachel closed the book, her hand still resting on the page to save her place.

"Excuse me," a timid man said as he handed me a pen still in its box. "This is for you and I wanted to buy a book if you could sign it for me?"

"Wow, that's so nice. I love it, thank you!" I gushed, my first ever gift from a fan. "Who do I make it out too?"

"Antonio."

"Antonio," I repeated. "I can't tell you how much this means to me. Thank you!"

He smiled shyly and left and I wished I could bottle all this love forever.

My phone suddenly buzzed and the smile faded as I read the text from my ex-husband.

You're a loser, a dead beat. What kind of mother leaves their kids?

Portsmouth, New Hampshire   June 13, 2015

Getting out of the car, I took a deep breath, took a picture of my first store, and thought, this is it. Weeks ago, my life was over. Weeks ago, I was crying on my couch after I'd seen the text message of another woman on my ex-husband's phone. He lied to me and I told him I'd do anything to save our sinking ship.

He left anyway. My neighbor tried to console me, but I wouldn't leave the house. She'd mix me a drink and put it on my doorstep while I got out of bed, turned off the porch lights to retrieve it in my underwear and t-shirt, sucked it down in one shot, and cried myself to sleep.

I was so afraid to go inside the store, but I had no choice now. My new life was in motion. I had made the appointment. I had shown up. And I was reborn into the unknown. It was go time. Sink or swim. And I wasn't ready to sink just yet.

Good Luck ☺, Sarah Louise texted me.

My hands shook a little as I texted a smiley face back and stuffed the phone into my purse. Sarah Louise loved to plan everything out. She was the exact opposite of me, calm, cool, and calculated. I, on the other hand, talked myself out of everything if I thought about it too long. Diving in was the only way.

"I'm the author," I said as I checked in with the cashier.

She didn't seem to mind that I was unable to remember who I'd spoken with originally or what I was supposed to do at all as she shook my hand.

"Let me show you your table. Follow me. If you want anything from the café just let me know."

"I'd love a coffee. Iced mocha?"

"I'll bring it to you."

Sitting down at my table, I placed my Sharpies neatly in front of me and stared at the stacks of books. It was eleven A.M., show time.

"Dixie?" I gasped when my aunt walked through the door holding my book.

"You look great, girl," she said as she hugged me.

"You too." I knew I sounded lame, but she was my idol growing up, more eloquent and poised than Jackie Kennedy. "At my work they call it the Divorce Diet. I cried so much when he left."

"Whatever they call it, you look great and you just keep doing what you're doing."

I always wanted to be doing what she was doing. She'd been married to my uncle for over twenty years now, probably even longer, and the way they looked at each other, even when they didn't agree, made me want to find what they had. But it didn't turn out that way.

"This is huge," she said as she held up my book. "Huge."

"Thank you. That's huge coming from you since you know Dan Brown and Stephen King."

"I don't know Stephen King," she shook her head. "He lives at the bottom of the hill, there's a difference."

"That's something," I shrugged.

"Joe keeps wanting to offer him a ride and I tell him, are you crazy? Drive faster!"

"Some of his stuff is amazing. I almost threw up when I read *Misery* because I could picture the gory stuff so clearly, and *On Writing* made me sad it when it was over."

Dixie grimaced like the very idea of Stephen King freaked her out, but Stephen King had the vision to write, even as a young boy, and had the support from his mother, and later in life, his wife. My only support from my husband was "What time is dinner?" and the only inspiration that I could remember came from a book mark I'd received in fourth grade that said "Writer's Award" that I couldn't find the heart to throw away. Something about the bookmark told me I was going to write a book someday, even though my writing wasn't ever good enough to be read aloud by the teacher. Those assignments bored me anyway.

I came full circle a few months after I'd left the military. I was on a bus for a job as a movie extra and the young man next to me dressed in a suit shared with me that he'd written self-help books and that it was the easiest genre to write because it was guaranteed to sell. All I had to do was be an expert in one subject, he'd said. It stumped me because all I had was being worldly. I knew a little bit about everything.

"I'm a little nervous," I said. "I'm an air traffic controller pretending to be a writer."

"You be whatever you have to be and call it whatever you want, but look at you, you're doing it. Forget him. Pfft, I can't believe all that you've done, military, written a book, and this? This is just the beginning for you, you'll see."

"Thank you, Dixie. It means a lot to me."

"Knock 'em dead, kid." She smiled when a woman in a big yellow sun hat picked up a copy of my book. "I love you and I'll see you later." She blew me a kiss and ducked out the door.

"Is this you on the cover?" the woman asked.

"Yes. It's from when I was in the Air Force and went overseas after 9/11."

"Thank you so much for your service," she said as she flipped through the pages. "I've been looking for a summer read and I'm sure my husband would love it, too. Can you sign it for him?"

"I'd love to." I pulled the cap off the Sharpie. "Who do I make it out to?"

"Raymond."

"Raymond," I repeated and signed my name with a smiley face. "I hope he loves it."

"I'm sure he will. He was in the Army and he reads anything and everything and then we switch books and talk about it. Raymond!" The woman called her husband over and said, "Raymond, this is…"

"Jen."

"…Jen and she just signed a book for you. Isn't that wonderful?"

"Thank you, young lady," he said. "If Nancy is raving about you then I'm sure we won't be able to put it down. If you don't mind, I need to steal her away for a moment."

"Good luck, Jen."

"Thank you! Enjoy the book," I called after them, and caught the eye of the employee standing behind the Nook counter a few feet away.

"Am I doing it right? This is my first signing."

"You're doing great," he smiled. "Some authors just sit there and don't say anything and some walk around the store. It's your call. Whatever you want to do, but if you're that happy with everyone, you're going to be fine. I was so impressed with you, when you get a minute, I'd like you to sign a copy for me, too."

I was floored. And then it truly hit me. I really had reclaimed the reigns. I fell and I got up again and was now in front of my very own poster with my very own book after months of working my tail off, coordinating and networking with anyone I could come in contact with. Like a domino, it only took one little push to start the chain reaction to set a new course for my life.

I inhaled the smell of books. Who knew books smelled so good?

"Are you the author JG Debs?" a woman approached me. "I thought I remembered reading that you were going to be here. You're the girl in the story, right?"

"Yes," I couldn't believe she'd heard about me. I could get used to this.

"Will you sign it?"

"I'd love to," I smiled. "Who do I make it out to?"

Chicago-Midway June 13, 2015

"Hi," I said pointing at the middle seat shyly. "I'm there."

"Oh." The man stood up. "Great. I'm Jim."

"Jen." I buckled my seatbelt surprised, at how chatty this guy was. I usually didn't like talking to strangers on a plane, but what the hell else was I going to do? The man leaning against the window was half asleep. "So what do you do, Jim?"

"I sell sprockets."

"Sprockets like bolts?"

"Yeah."

"That's the most random thing I've ever heard. And you have to travel for that?"

"All the time. I'm on the road nine months out of the year."

"Have you seen the movie 'Up in the Air'?"

"Yeah," he smirked. "It's kinda like that, but not really, nah."

"So you know all the flight attendants?"

"Sometimes," he laughed.

"I just met a woman in the terminal who sells furniture and she also travels a lot. She called herself the "Queen of Midway" since she flies there at least three times a week. I didn't realize traveling was still so popular for companies these days. Your family doesn't mind?"

"Ah, they're used to it. I've been doing it for twelve years and I'm home for all the holidays so I can't complain either."

"You must see some crazy stuff. Tell me the craziest story."

"I can give you strange. I don't know if it's crazy. This one time I was flying in the middle seat like you. You're the best middle seat flyer, by the way."

"Thanks. Not that I have a choice. Usually, all the other seats are taken because I'm usually running late. And I don't mind as long as I get on. I used to fly standby all the time growing up and that's like the worst game of chance when the flight is full."

"I can imagine." He nodded and went back to the story. "So, this woman, as soon as I sat down, folds down all the tables. It was a three-seat row like this. She lies across them, and says she's hung over and needs to sleep."

"She laid down on all the tables and they didn't break?"

"Nope."

"And she slept?"

"The entire flight. Reeked of alcohol, too. I've never seen anything like it," Jim said shaking his head.

"I don't believe it."

"I didn't believe it, either. But it's true, Scout's honor," he said, raising his hand.

"That's a pretty good story. And what do you do with the sprockets?"

"Conventions. Presentations for different companies, things like that. I used to fly with someone, but we got on each other's nerves. He wanted to do one thing and I wanted to do another, so now we travel separately. What do you do?"

"I'm an air traffic controller turned author and I'm on book tour."

"What's the book called? I'm always looking for a good book."

"*Back in Two Weeks*," I said, and he fished out a pen and paper from his briefcase.

"Got it. Well, Jen, I must say, it's been a pleasure."

"Thanks," I laughed. "I hope you sell a lot of sprockets."

"I hope you sell a lot of books."

Las Vegas, Nevada   January 9, 2015

If I could live my life anyway I could without consequences, I would go all the way, like Hunter S. Thompson. I would light a cigarette and snort coke and chase it all with a shot and forget about the world and write marvelous books and win awards and make lots of money.

But I was not him. And I was never going to be him. I was me. And I was sitting in a grocery store parking lot, avoiding my reflection of my oversized aviators poorly covering my tear streaked face in the rearview mirror.

Why the hell was no one else crying in public? Fifty percent of marriages ended in divorce, people died every day, and yet I was the only one who had to leave the house and get groceries and didn't have her shit together?

"I'm fine," I wanted to tell people as they stared at me crying over my grocery list. But maybe I was paranoid. Maybe they didn't even notice me at all.

I stared at the groceries in my cart and wished I wasn't so god damned responsible all the time. I wanted to hit the pause button on life because it was coming at me like a never-ending freight train. Why couldn't life's lessons arrive a tad more delicately?

I'd been planning a cruise to celebrate our eleven year anniversary. He'd been planning our divorce.

"I thought we were going to be together forever," I'd said to him after we finally decided to split the finances.

Even then, I couldn't sit still. I paced back and forth and watched as he smiled at the computer screen. Twelve years of savings split in two, his half now to support him and his girlfriend. What a waste.

"So did I," he'd shrugged.

Checkmate.

The death of our marriage flashed before me, my best friend now a total stranger. I wanted to hate him, but I couldn't. For the last few months, as he dragged this out, I even waffled back and forth with the idea if he changed his mind, would I take him back? Even though I wanted to save the marriage for our kids.

I knew deep down I couldn't. Not after all he'd done. It wasn't so much the divorce, but how tastelessly he went about leaving me.

I almost laughed as he sat there with his Clark Kent glasses I'd picked out for him. He really did look like Superman I thought. Why the hell did I marry Superman if I had always been in love with Batman?

Back in the car, I turned on the radio and listened as Laura McBride told of her upcoming book tour on NPR. She was a local author who taught at the university and talked about how she had locked herself in her room for three months and banged out her book and never looked back.

I wanted to be like her. That was the frame of mind I had to get into.

I am Hunter S. Thompson and I am Laura McBride and I'm gonna do this was my new mantra. I'm going on book tour. I'm getting my ass off the couch and I'm going to stop crying and feeling sorry for myself, and I'm going to be the best mother I can for my kids.

All I had to do was find one person who wouldn't say no to me.

Las Vegas, Nevada   January 8, 2015

"It was in December," Sal reminded me.

As I waited for the rest of his speech, I glanced around at all of us on the couch, his mom, dad, and me, Sal's arms crossed in defiance or lack of interest or both, even though he'd called this conference.

"You're the one who said you wanted a divorce, and how many times did I have to listen to it? How many times did I tell you, *careful what you wish for?*"

"You know I didn't mean it," I pleaded, more to his parents, who were actually looking at me. "Tell him I didn't mean it. You know I love your son more than anything," I said looking at his father.

"So what the problem?" his dad asked, his Lebanese accent still strong after twenty-something years in the States. "Why you call me here?"

"He said he wanted you here." I pointed at my husband, who had orchestrated the meeting and of course did not said much at all.

"You want to talk? Talk," his father said to him, but Sal said nothing.

"I can't do this, all of this, anymore." I said. "It's too much. I mean, I'm taking care of the kids and working and he sleeps in every day. He can't get to work on time, ever, and we never even see each other, and all he does is complain to me that I'm complaining, and how long does his mother have to live here? I'm sorry, but it's true." I looked at her, but she didn't bat an eye.

"You know you have two kids and you have to take care of them," his father went on. "And you don't have to blame it on his mother."

"Ok, but now it's too much. I can't keep taking care of everyone by myself." Even he knew his ex-wife was overbearing, over-demanding, and ungrateful, but wasn't going to bother to say it to her face.

"What too much?" My father-in-law looked at me blankly. What the hell did a man know about being a full-time mother with a full-time demanding job and a non-existent husband who snuck out of the house until one A.M., thinking I didn't know about it? "Before, when you met, you give. A lot. But I notice then it's less and less."

"How much more than everything can I possibly give? Is this a fucking joke?"

"Why you swearing?"

"I'm swearing because I can't believe what I'm hearing. Look. He called this meeting for you to come here and it's me yelling, as usual. I didn't even want to say anything and now I'm saying it. I can't do it all. I can't. I ask for help and he leaves the room. It's like on purpose or something. And his mom, it was supposed to be one month. One. Now it's eight. For the third time she has moved here and out stayed her welcome. I got her a job, I wrote a letter on her behalf stating that she was an excellent, motivated worker and she didn't even show up!"

"Sit down!" his father shouted at me.

"I will not sit down! This is my house that I worked for and I'm tired of everyone disrespecting me and not giving a shit! I like myself and yes, I might be an asshole, but I work hard and I have done a lot for this family. A lot!"

"Sit down!" He leaped up. "You call me here and I'm here. You not talk to me like that!"

I walked away, made it to the stairs before I reminded myself that we were at the end and I couldn't run away now. I was serious about saving my marriage, and if we all had to duke it out, so be it. It was worth it for my kids because this was how I grew up. My parents divorced when I was three and my brother two. My son was four and my daughter one, and I wanted more for them than being lugged around from one house to another.

"Let me tell you something! I never liked you..."

"What?" My face dropped.

"...He said he want to marry you and I said okay, but I knew not good. And then you fight and when you come to me I say nothing. I was always fair to you, but now this."

"I had to come to you because he never listened," I said, tears streaming down my face. "You know how much I love him. How can you say that to me?"

"When you tell me something then I ask him and he say it's not how it is. But I didn't say anything. I'm sick of listening to your fights. You need to work it out, you two."

"Say something!" I screamed at my husband. "You had something to say and now you won't say it!"

"No, no, no!" His mother exploded to life. "I've been listening long enough to this. For months I've been listening to you fighting and I've had enough, too. You are to blame and you are to blame." She pointed at her son, then me. "It's gone on long enough. Both of you hurt each other on purpose and try to make the other one look bad. I've tried to talk to both of you and no one listens to me and I just sit here like a fly on the wall, day in and day out."

About to tell her she was right, she looked at me and changed the game.

"I'm not finished. You, my son, deserve someone better than her."

About the Author

JG Debs is the author of *Back in Two Weeks* and *Millennial Cookbook: How the Guy next door learned to cook*. She lives in Las Vegas, where she has worked at McCarran Airport for almost twelve years. She has a Bachelor's Degree in Psychology and a Master's Degree from Embry Riddle in Aeronautical Science. Her daughter and son light up her life.

www.ingramcontent.com/pod-product-compliance
Lightning Source LLC
Chambersburg PA
CBHW031430290426
44110CB00011B/608